APOCALYPSE 2027: ANTICHRIST UNMASKED

APOCALYPSE 2027: ANTICHRIST UNMASKED

The scriptural case for the Global Antichrist

PETER JENSEN

Quanonical Books
Coppell, TX

Special discounts are available on bulk purchases by corporations, associations, and others. For details, contact the publisher at the address given below.
Quanonical Books
450 S. Denton Tap Rd #2347, Coppell, TX 75019 USA

ISBN: 978-1-7322232-1-9
eBook ISBN: 978-1-7322232-0-2

Library of Congress Control Number: 2018940615

Printed in the United States of America

10 9 8 7 6 5 4 3 2 1

First Edition

Dedication

This book is dedicated to all those who choose to obey their consciences before God. I dedicate this to all people of goodwill who labor without thought of reward in God's vineyard, who stand up and do what is right irrespective of where it may lead them.

"What has been will be again, what has been done will be done again; there is nothing new under the sun."
Ecclesiastes 1:9

Contents

Foreword

THE APOCALYPTIC PROPHECIES OF ISAIAH are rarely referenced by Bible prophecy experts but they are a goldmine of truths that cannot be dismissed. The prophecies of Isaiah are not always allegorical or symbolic but are *literally* true, from Christ's manner of birth(born to a virgin), his method of redeeming Man(through his own suffering Servantship and criminal manner of death by scourging and crucifixion) and the just punishment meted out to all the kings of the earth at the time of the His Second Coming.

The last of these has been mostly dismissed as figurative in the past, considering that Isaiah was not aware of kingdoms beyond the Middle Eastern or Mediterranean region. If the first two were described literally, it follows that the last MUST also be literally true.

There is a tendency of self-styled prophecy experts to interpret Bible prophecies in the light of current events, even if short-term. Just think - how many prophecies that you have read over the last 100 years have come true ?

Sure, but the return of the Jewish peoples to Israel was pointed out to us AFTER it happened, exactly as in Ezekiel's vision of the dry bones coming together(***Ezekiel 37***). Why haven't later prophetic interpretations after that come true? The angel who spoke to the prophet Daniel gives us a clue.

*"And he said, "Go your way, Daniel, for these words are concealed and sealed up **until the end time." Daniel 12:9** (NASB)*

As is explained later in this book, we are entering the final decade of the Lord's return. And if the time of the end is towards the next decade, of what use are older interpretations of the end times even if they were made 50 or even 15 years ago? This book will only use two simple rules to understand prophecy, one of them given to us by the great Biblical scholar Dr David L. Cooper.

Dr Cooper gave us the Golden rule of Interpretation, namely "When the plain sense of scripture makes common sense, **seek no other sense;** Therefore take every word at its primary, ordinary, usual, literal meaning unless the facts of the immediate context, studied in the light of related passages .... indicate clearly otherwise"

An excellent example of this is *literally* interpreting the Messiah verse in **Zechariah 9:9** "Rejoice greatly, O daughter of Zion! Shout in triumph, O daughter of Jerusalem! Behold, your king is coming to you; He is just and endowed with salvation, Humble, and mounted on a donkey, Even on a colt, the foal of a donkey."

Did anyone in Israel think that the future Messiah, the King of kings would come riding on a donkey with a foal walking by its side? Which other king in history has come ever so humbly?

Yet that is exactly what happened when Jesus rode into Jerusalem, with the common people singing Hosannas as He arrived. *(Matthew 21:2-5)*

The second rule is the maximal use of corroborating witnesses just as in a court of law - a witness whose testimony supports or confirms testimony that is given by another witness. This witness will be served by the Jewish prophets like Isaiah, Daniel, Ezekiel, Zechariah and others corroborating each other's prophecies in many surprising places, as you will see in this book.

This book will aim to re-frame apocalyptic prophecy interpretation in the last 100 years and yet show today how the Bible scholars of old were right on point. The diligent student of eschatology might have known that there was more than we have been told these past few decades.

What I understood from the 1990s was this - from the fall of the atheistic Soviet Union in early 1991, the world would be given exactly 40 years to come back to God. At communism's highest realization, fully over 60% of the population of the world lived under harsh atheistic communist or socialist regimes that were modeled after the mother lode - the Soviet Union, making it the defacto greatest empire in history even more than the British.

Yet the Soviet Union itself collapsed so suddenly and precipitously that it was no longer seen anymore in history. This singular event alone should have reminded human beings of God's awesome power at work but they continued as if nothing had changed. God was calling us back to Himself and we were not listening.

What this book will tell us - the old and the entirely new

There is no attempt to exactly time the Rapture or the return of the Lord in this book as some prophecy experts are still wont to do. We will not get into debating yet again pre-tribulation vs mid-tribulation vs pre-wrath Rapture timing. Better still: Expect the worst, hope for the best, maybe you'll end up with something wonderful in between!

The timing of that signless event is not for us to know, as you have seen with several wrong calls from William Miller in the 19th century even onto Harold Camping in the 21st. Neither are we ever going to know the exact hour or even day or year of the Lord's Coming.

After 1900 years of speculation, we will also finally discover the meaning of the code given to Antichrist by the Apostle John in the Book of Revelation. Yes, this is the real deal! And in about 10 years I promise you will also be able to identify the Antichrist even before he is revealed. To be forewarned is to be forearmed. I challenge any atheist to predict a future road map like that given to us by the prophets, freely available from God's Word.

The book will also cover the exact buildup and the absolute inevitability of the coming of the Antichrist's short-lived kingdom in the next decade. To this end I hope it will be both interesting and something you will look forward to reading. This book is not a book of doom and gloom but a book of hope with a road-map to how we will get there, taken straight out of the Bible.

> "Come, let us return to the Lord.
> He has torn us to pieces
>   but he will heal us;
> he has injured us
>   but he will bind up our wounds.
> After two days he will revive us;
>   on the third day he will restore us,
>   that we may live in his presence. **Hosea 6:1-2** (NIV)

Archaeologists in Israel have recently found a 2,700-year clay seal mark that may bear the signature of the Biblical Prophet Isaiah, at the foot of the southern wall of Jerusalem's Temple Mount. It was found next to an artifact that bore the seal of the Judean king Hezekiah. It is only fitting that this book is dedicated to the same Prophet who not only gave us the historically singular manner of Christ's birth and the means He would employ to save Man not once but once more, coming again in glory at the end of Time.

Last but not least, I am greatly indebted to my spiritual mentors the late Don Campbell and Dr Ken Taylor of the Dallas Theological Seminary for their wonderful insights and teaching these past decades.

CHAPTER 1
Is the Apocalypse finally on hold ?

WITH PRO-CHRISTIAN PRESIDENT Donald J. Trump in power as the commander in chief of the United States, is the coming Apocalypse now officially on hold ? With the EU disintegrating as we speak, is the apocalypse or "unveiling" of the "revived Roman empire" at a standstill ?

Can we all sigh in relief as the Arab Sunni nations of the Middle East align with the United States and Israel against Shiite Iran and the vastly impotent Shiite Syrian regime? Ezekiel 38 surely talks of some of Middle Eastern nations refusing to take part in this alignment against Israel. But there's also the question of Psalm 83 with those same missing nations, exactly unfulfilled till today.

While the nominally Sunni government of Turkey seems to be aligning with the Syrian government, Turkey is still a NATO member. If that changes tomorrow, the Germans and the French are individually powerful enough to hold their NATO neighbor in check, without even involving the United States.

Shiite Iran is caught in an impasse over Jerusalem that does not seem to be moving forward as they want with additional resistance from the staunchly Sunni Arab countries. Would the so-called "Islamic Antichrist" have the solid bust of a Sunni, the bronzed thighs of a Shia and the clay feet of an Ismaili ? Humor aside, difficulties will be pointed out next to show that we are actually heading away from the predicted Islamic Antichrist.

So is the Apocalypse itself finally on hold ? You will see why this is not the case and that is simply the first step of many more to come for the world to get to the point of no return. Indeed we are already past the point of no return. There are several events on the political, religious and technological horizons that are actually aligning well with each other.

Note that in this book I will spell and name the final Antichrist capitalized as opposed to other little antichrists that will also be mentioned in this book. For example, Hitler and Stalin were forms of antichrist but neither was the final Antichrist. These last two especially were however radical warnings of things to come.

Trump reelected as POTUS in 2020 - A prelude

Under the common sense pro-American policies of President Donald J. Trump, the popularity of the generous tax cuts and Trump's pressure on the Republicans to go nuclear to address thorny issues, we predict that he will be re-elected in 2020 as the economy of the United States continues to improve even in the midst of new trade wars.

At present North Korea both threatens as well as baits and switches on partial nuclear deals with the US till the next elections in 2020, hoping to ease off punitive sanctions on their country till Trump leaves. Only problem is Trump isn't going anywhere.

After Trump's reelection in 2020, the increased paranoia within the North Korean ranks will give them no recourse then but to show their hostile capabilities to pre-empt an expected attack by the United States, after a period of deceitful impasse with the West.

The overheating of the world economies, rising debt, increased inflation, hostile trade wars, unsustainable stock market prices, North Korean nuclear arming of Iran and an opportunistic warning attack on pacifist Japan will finally lead to war and drop the world economy off the cliff after 12 good years of economic prosperity.

The so-called Shemitah(seventh) year of 2015 and many blood moons came and went with no impact on the United States whatsoever, as it had on Israel in years past. Many moons later, how will the Apocalypse unfold ?

CHAPTER 2
Why the Antichrist is not from the European Union

THE OFFICIAL EUROPEAN JOKE GOES SOMETHING LIKE
THIS: A European paradise is when you are invited to an official
lunch. At the lunch you are welcomed by an Englishman. Food is
prepared by a Frenchman, an Italian puts you in the mood and
everything is organized by a German.

The European version of hell is again being invited to an
official lunch. But here you are welcomed by a Frenchman. Food
is prepared by an Englishman, a German puts you in the mood
but, don't worry, everything is organized by an Italian.

There is a newer version of this European hell. You are
invited to an official lunch. But this time there is no food because
the Englishman simply decides not to show up.

There is really no verse in the Bible that points specifically
to only the nations of Europe running the globe. The islands of
Tarshish(**Isaiah 23**) mentioned in the Bible are understood by
Biblical scholars to denote the lands of Europe across the
Mediterranean sea from the Middle East. The trade with Tyre (a
coastal city of Lebanon) and long sea trips made by King
Solomon's men to Tarshish are also mentioned.

"For the king (Solomon) had ships which went to Tarshish
with the servants of Huram; *once every three years* the ships of
Tarshish came bringing gold and silver, ivory and apes and

peacocks." *2 Chronicles 9:21 (NASB)*

Elsewhere in *Ezekiel 38,* Tarshish is mentioned as standing by accusingly as a Middle Eastern war of many nations erupts with Israel.

So rather than force the EU into the ten horns, we have to approach this from a decidedly much better way - we will actually name the regions that will form the 10 horns of the Antichrist !

The arrangement of the horns will be detailed in a later chapter of this book, derived from a historical meeting that preceded the modern European union. Feel free to skip to the chapter in this book that names and maps the 10 horns.

The European Union(EU) today is currently a political and economic union of 27 countries with its well paid political elite based out of Brussels. When the European Communities of six nations was proposed and eventually formed, Europe was just emerging out of the destruction of World War II.

The widespread devastation suffered by most of Europe prompted politicians to get together and create a political and economic rulebook that would prevent any of the formerly largest empires - German, British, French, Spanish, Portuguese and many others from re-emerging as a threat to Europe.

The European Union was finally proposed in 1992 at Maastricht (the Netherlands) to offer Europeans a single citizenship. Even today, Turkey which straddles both Europe and Asia has attempted and failed to obtain EU citizenship for itself.

At first the future of the EU looked promising. With the highest GDP of any nation or group of nations in history, the EU was set to dominate politically and economically. However cracks began to appear in a mere two decades with a trillion dollars in debt due from just Spain, Italy, Greece and Portugal. And Greece, Republic of Ireland and Portugal ended up getting further massive financial bailouts from the EU.

The last straw that literally broke the camel's back was the sudden in-pouring of huge numbers of immigrants from third world countries in the Middle East such as Syria, Afghanistan in South Asia and others. The bureaucrats in Brussels and the socialist parties did not forecast the possibility of an ongoing citizens' revolt against this unchecked flow in different European nations.

Today there is a new resurgence of nationalist parties on the political scene. With the exit of Britain and now even Sweden, Denmark, Hungary and others threatening to leave soon, the European Union is fast crumbling. Give or take another five years, there might be no European Union.

The endless failures of qualified majority voting

The Single European Act(SEA) eliminated the national veto and replaced it with qualified majority voting of member states. This meant that too many times smaller individual nations in the Union got outvoted on issues. (Note: this will be important in a later chapter of this book). And what is the SEA?

For a moment, imagine the United States as a European-like Union of several "countries" like California and New York. By virtue of their massive populations, these two "countries" could have easily set the laws and values for the rest of the Union, if the founding fathers of the United States had not foreseen such an exact situation 250 years ago!

The founding fathers including Benjamin Franklin set the same number of senate votes for each state, small or large in the union, creating an automatic limit on the powers of the House run by larger states, against the population based voting plan proposed by James Madison. The European union on the other hand has none of those protections for smaller states. Brussels, the capital of the EU was accused of interfering in and strong arming individual smaller and less powerful European governments for its own agenda.

And at some point analysts predict that Germany and France, the two most powerful countries will also possibly be the last men standing in the ill-fated European Union. There are already growing economic tensions between north and south Europe.

Europe is turning slowly into a ghetto of confusing atheistic and progressive ideas. It has dumped and censored God in the interest of so-called "human rights" for those who embrace the perverse.

If the EU collapses from within in the next few years as political and financial analysts today predict, how will the "revived Roman empire" come about ? Does the revived Roman empire refer to the EU or to the West in whole ?

CHAPTER 3
Why the Antichrist is not from the Islamic Middle East

IN FEBRUARY 2015, ON A WINTRY BEACH IN LIBYA, a group of ISIS members marched 23 Egyptian Coptic Christians to the edge of the waters of the Mediterranean Sea. Held in place by a line of black-clad, knife-wielding captors, the Christian men were forced to kneel while the executioners reached down and slashed their necks. And yet these brave but doomed men were heard calling out to the Lord even as they were barbarically executed.

And in an explicit bid to emphasize the growing reach of the group and its proximity to European shores, the mass execution was videotaped and described as taking place on Libya's Mediterranean coast, "south of Rome."

Today at the end of December 2017 a mere two years later, under the leadership of Trump and with similar work from Russia's Vladimir Putin, ISIS is almost completely destroyed. Their Islamic prophecy that the world would end in Raqqa(Syria) where they had their headquarters is now in tatters and they are forced today to run for their lives as Western and allied Middle Eastern Muslim forces decimate them by the day.

Syrian and Iraqi Muslims who have suffered from the actions of ISIS are as much horrified and traumatized by the actions of the group as much as the rest of the world, seeing them as a danger and blot on Islam.

Today, some people live in the West in fear of the Islamic

hordes invading their country through mass immigration. They see a different culture that appears barbaric and marginalizes women. They see imminent danger from Islam to the West.

There is little spirituality in Islam the West can identify with. The culture appears alien to Christians brought up in the love of God and the vision of God as a loving merciful father to undeserving children. Yet Jesus has always told Christians what to fear more than those who can kill the body - we are to fear the loss of our own soul, something NO radical Islamist will ever be able to take away from us.

*"Do not fear those who kill the body but are unable to kill the soul; but rather fear Him who is able to destroy both soul and body in hell." **Matthew 10:28** (NASB)*

The origin of the beliefs of Mohammad regarding Jesus and His return

Contrary to popular beliefs of Mohammad knowing little of Jesus before he received his revelations "in the spirit" at a cave in the Arabian desert, he was already exposed to heretical Christian beliefs prevalent in Arabia at the time, from a close relative.

This relative was his own cousin, a Nestorian Christian by the name Waraqah ibn(son of) Nawfal. Waraqah ibn Nawfal was the paternal first cousin of Khadija, the first and much older wife of the Islamic prophet Muhammad. Waraqah and Khadija were also first cousins twice removed of Muhammad.

The youngest (and last) wife of Mohammad, Aisha also shows us the importance of Waraqah in supporting the Prophet's revelations, in her own words :

"The Prophet returned to Khadija while his heart was beating rapidly. She took him to Waraqa ibn Nawfal who was a

Christian convert and used to read the Gospel in Arabic. Waraqah asked (the Prophet), "What do you see?" When he told him, Waraqah said, "That is the same angel whom Allah sent to the Prophet) Moses. Should I live till you receive the Divine Message, I will support you strongly." (Narrated 'Aisha: Volume 4, Book 55, Number 605)

Which "gospel" is mentioned here is not known since by this time in the seventh century there were also many Gnostic versions of the gospels available in Arabia.

Waraqah was in reality a Nestorian priest and is revered in Islamic tradition for being one of the first to believe in the prophecy of Muhammad. Nestorianism stressed the independence of the divine and human natures of Christ and, in effect, suggested that they were two persons loosely united. In modern times they are represented by the Church of the East, or the Assyrian Church.

However to a Christian, splitting the divine and human nature of Jesus Christ is heresy. It would mean that Jesus did not die on the cross for Christians as only His "body" suffered. If taken to its logical conclusion, Nestorianism denies salvation and redemption.

All Christians however believe that Jesus Christ is both fully human and fully God. Jesus Himself declares this in the Gospels identifying Himself both the Son of Man and Son of God, while being One with God the Father. This is a Christian mystery, an article of faith stated explicitly by Jesus Christ.

Why there will never be a single Islamic caliphate
Islam unlike Christianity is mostly just two major denominations - Sunni and Shia with the Sunni far outnumbering the Shia. The rest of the denominations in Islam further pale in significance to these two major yet irreconcilable players in the Islamic world. A

single Islamic caliph therefore would have to be Sunni or Shia, and neither Iran nor the majority of the Arab world will accept the other. So the question of a single Islamic "Caliph" is impossible.

Any so-called Islamic Antichrist with ambitions of world conquest will be a minor player under the thumb of the major world powers that are Russia and China. It is clear today that the Iranians are firmly in the Russian orbit, and in some places such as Syria, completely depend on the Russians and their advanced technology to smooth the way for their domination of Syria and even Iraq.

So Iran is at best a minor bit player and is more existentially dangerous to Israel than it is to the West. The existential danger to the West is more from the atheist CPC (Communist Party of China) and also to some extent from Russia that has been forever at odds with the West.

The facts today speak for themselves. The Middle East is a group of mostly poor and a few oil rich countries of the Arabian Gulf that gleam of gold but are still firmly entrenched in the Third world despite all that pomp and glitter. Today the black gold that made parts of the Middle East prosperous is also running out quickly and there is mild panic setting in among the oil rich sheikhdoms.

When that happens more revolutions will be fomented in each country that will make Syria look like a walk in the park. In other words Arab Spring 2.0 is coming. Leaving more for China and even Russia to exploit as the US actively disengages from Syria, Iraq and the rest of the Middle East, continuing however to support Israel from afar.

Al-Mahdi in the Sunni vs the Shia(Shiite) Islamic traditions

In Sunni beliefs, the figure of al-Mahdi simply refers to the very human Islamic caliph at any time. In the Shia tradition that came much later and is mostly concentrated in Iran with the Arab states of Iraq and Bahrain being exceptions, the figure of al-Mahdi is more supernatural in nature. In the Shiite tradition, the Mahdi is **"occulted"**, or hidden from believers for centuries till an appropriate time when he resurfaces in Iran to support Jesus(the Messiah) against the Antichrist.

Note that the Mahdi is **NOT** the Messiah in either tradition. The Twelver or *Imamiyyah* mullahs (so called after the long awaited Twelfth Shia Mahdi) making up most of Iran's government are currently watching a well outside Jamkaran mosque in Qom, Iran from where they believe this Mahdi will emerge. Note that it is not the Sunnis that are watching this well or for that matter care anything about Shiite beliefs.

Worldwide, the more influential Sunnis also outnumber Shiites nine to one. The Sunnis belonging to the original tradition of Mohammad consider these Shiite beliefs held in Iran as dangerously heretical to their own faith. The figure of al-Mahdi is not as important and sometimes even omitted in Sunni Islam. It is expected that the Mahdi will be known to Sunni Muslims only after he politically unites them, as a rightly guided caliph.

That is, in Sunni tradition, the caliph who achieves this unity will be considered a Mahdi, just as certain caliphs have already been considered Mahdis in prior Islamic history.

This Islamic unity itself is implausible in the near future or beyond given the tensions between the Sunni and the Shia as well as other minor branches of Islam. However the Sunni Muslims (as do the Shiites) do believe that Jesus(the Messiah) will come again. Mohammad himself mentions this in the Quran Surah (chapter) 43

"And (Jesus) shall be a Sign (for the coming of) the Hour (of Judgment): therefore have no doubt about the (Hour), but follow ye Me: this is a Straight Way." (Surah 43:61 in the Quran)

Other writings by Muslims from the Hadith or sayings of Mohammad also speak of the coming of Jesus against Dajjal(AntiChrist):

"In the meantime, while the Dajjal(Antichrist) will be busy doing (this) and this, Allah will send down the Messiah son of Mary (Jesus). He (Jesus) will descend in the eastern part of Damascus, near the white minaret (tower), dressed in the two yellowish garments, with his hands resting on the arms of two angels. When he will bend down his head, water drops will appear trickling down, and when he will raise it, it will appear as though pearl--like drops are rolling down. Any disbeliever whom the air of his breath reaches, and it will reach up to the last limit of his sight, will fall dead. Then, the son of Mary will go in pursuit of the Dajjal(Antichrist), and will overtake him at the gate of Lud , and will kill him." (Sahih Muslim, Tirmizi, Ibn Majah, a Hadith attributed to Mohammad)

While these details seem dramatic when elaborated thus in the Quran, the Christian will understand no such blow by blow details of the work of the Lord are necessary, because even starting from Genesis and unto Jesus Himself, it is clear that the Lord can speak any action into existence in the Bible and is nothing like ordinary human beings.

So these details seem superfluous at best and do not serve to educate the Christian believer. God is a perfect executor of His Word and does not miss any of His enemies at the end of Time!

Al-Mahdi in the Ahmadiyah Islamic tradition

Also it is clear from the above that neither Sunni nor Shia Muslims that together make about 99% of the Muslim population of the world consider the figure of al-Mahdi and the Messiah to be the same person. In both traditions Jesus is always the Messiah(of the Jews).

However there is another Islamic tradition considered heretical by both the Sunnis and Shias (to the point of extreme persecution in all Muslim countries today) that believe that al-Mahdi and Messiah are the same person. This is the Ahmadiyah tradition that was started in the Punjab in present day Pakistan by Mirza Ghulam Alam.

The followers of this tradition also follow other beliefs that mainstream Muslims consider heretic - namely, that Jesus was not taken away by God from the Cross and yet did not die of his injuries received from extensive scourging and crucifixion. According to Mirza, he later came down from the cross, nursed himself back to health and traveled to Kashmir in India where he lived out the rest of his life and was buried.

However to Christians who read the detailed Gospel accounts of the crucifixion it is clear that without treatment, Jesus would have eventually died from the intense scourging he received at the hands of Pontius Pilate. Indeed He dies too early on the cross partly from massive blood loss, for we are told this early passing surprises Pilate(**Mark 15:44**).

After all, crucifixion was a form of punishment crafted by the Romans to torture and kill the crucified unfortunate slowly and excruciatingly over days, serving as an additional deterrent to future enemies. It is clear from the Gospel accounts that Pilate finding no fault in Him, tried to let him go free by satisfying in part the blood lust of his accusers with an extensive scourging, later only giving into their demands for His full execution.

The Ahmadiyah beliefs are therefore far removed from the origins of Islam in the Middle East but these are only mentioned to avoid confusion with the major Islamic traditions and establish that the Mahdi and Messiah being One person is not a mainstream Islamic belief.

One of the few common beliefs that the Sunni, Shia and the other sects believe in is that the Mahdi will come from the family of the prophet Mohammad and that he will rule the unified Islamic caliphate for 7 years. Mohammad himself was to have said

"The Mahdi will be of my family, of the descendants of Fatimah (the Prophet's daughter)" (Sunan Abu Dawud).

Now consider this: King Abdullah II, the Sunni monarch of the Hashemite kingdom of Jordan is a 42nd generation direct descendant of Mohammad. Some Sunni quarters actually consider him to be the future Mahdi.

Even the late Iraqi despot Saddam Hussein co-opted the symbolism of the Mahdi appearing on a white horse by having himself painted on a white horse all over Baghdad, thus laying claim to be a Mahdi in his own right. Neither King Abdullah nor Saddam Hussein, both being Sunnis had dared lay any claim to any supernatural powers whatsoever, unlike the later Shia version of the Mahdi.

Problems with the Hadiths - they are not the Quran!

If you have played the communication game as a child, you are aware that the message transmitted orally from the first person to the second in line is rarely that which is retransmitted to the next person and so on. By the time the last person receives the message passed down, it might end up drastically different from the first person's original communication. That's usually part of the fun!

An exactly similar problem arises with the hadiths or sayings of Mohammad. Increasing this difficulty is the fact that the Quran was put down in writing only about 150 years after the death of Mohammad. Contrast this with the 4 gospels of the New Testament all of which were available in the very first century of Christ's crucifixion.

There are other problems due to these many hadiths attributed to Mohammad. These sayings of Mohammad(not directly in the Quran itself) but orally repeated by followers regarding "breaking the cross" and "killing the pig" seem to have been more on Mohammad's or his followers' wish-lists than anything Jesus himself would want to do.

Jesus can scarcely be imagined going about having crosses broken and swine liquidated, for any reason. For these reasons above, we will not go further into these many hadiths, or sayings of Mohammad, that are not part of the Quran itself.

Many of these sets of hadiths or sayings do not agree always with each other causing different Muslims to favor one or the other at any time. For example, there are many places where Sahih Muslim hadiths do not agree with the accounts in the Sahih Bukhari hadiths and other Islamic hadiths.

Since these hadiths are mostly not found in the Quran itself, it is impossible to know for sure what Mohammad actually said, outside of the Quran.

Political and demographic reality of Islam in the Middle East and the West

Is a future Islamic leader or self-proclaimed Caliph the Antichrist? This is what some not too long ago thought. Is this enigmatic figure for many years once seen to be Khomeini or Saddam or even Gaddafi or OBL (when they were alive) the final Antichrist ? We'll discuss why that is not likely given the news today and the long divisions within Islam.

First, all Muslims are not Arabs or live in the Middle Eastern region of Asia. There is a wide diversity of Muslims over the world, with Saudi Arabia, Egypt, Iran, Turkey and Indonesia being major representatives of these wide deviations.

Saudi Arabia is rooted in the strict Salafi or Wahabi Sunni tradition - an extremely conservative interpretation of the Quran and the Sunnah. Turkey though majority Sunni is secular in an Islamic religious sense as its government aims to paint itself as being tolerant of the Alevi (Shiite Muslim) minority and other minor branches of Islam. *This is in stark contrast with the Saudi Arabian persecution of the Shiite Muslims in that country.*

Turkey's "secular" stance is not a recent development, but deeply rooted in history. The Turks belong to the less restrictive Sunni Hanefi-Maturidi tradition that matured in the urban environments of Baghdad, and spread to Istanbul, Cairo and Islamabad, where many faiths coexisted. The Indonesians of South east Asia and the Egyptians of North Africa are similar to the Turks in religious outlook.

Interestingly Saudi Arabia, Egypt and Turkey each consider themselves in the role of Islam's leader, in their very different traditions. "Secular" Turkey is also not as inimical to Iran as is Wahabi Saudi Arabia, having decided not to infuriate their Shiite minority. The mostly Sunni nations of Central Asia having adopted the "secular" Sunni traditions of Turkey are also not inimical to Shiite Iran. Azerbaijan is also a majority Shia nation.

Turkey also sees itself as the successor of the Ottoman empire, a fact not lost on many of the Arab countries south of it, including Saudi Arabia and the Gulf Arab nations that received their independence from the Turkish Ottoman empire a hundred years ago, after World War 1 and a previous hundred years of resistance against the Ottoman Turks.

The chance that these Arab nations will once again align with their former Turkish rulers is therefore almost insignificant, simply for the fear of becoming a pawn in Turkey's regional games in the Middle East, or diluting their own Arab traditions. Its complicated.

To understand the broad reason why the world will never see a global Islamic caliphate, take a further look at the economies of the Middle East. Every one of them is supported either on oil or agriculture. There is neither a knowledge or diversified industrial economy as in the West with its own continuous research and development feeding today's knowledge based economy.

Having lived in the Middle East myself in the 1970s and 1980s I have seen firsthand how self-limited in power these countries are in spite of their massive purchases of Western or Russian hardware.

We should also know that from the historical example of Iraq's Saddam that it is virtually impossible to simply buy your way to worldwide military power. There must always be a national industry that undertakes to develop an offensive and defensive capability that is not dependent on other powers.

This is not available anywhere in the Middle East except in Israel. The only other economy in Asia that has massive research and development in the armaments industry is in China.

Islam's own dreams of dominating the rest of the world is already in the dust, never to rise again. Even the stated religious aim of using newer refugees in the West to slowly out-breed the native Westerners is many decades in the making.

It is estimated that only 0.1% (or 1 in 1000) of Muslim increase in the West and elsewhere is through conversion or preaching to non-Muslims. Additionally Europeans are starting to realize that the current levels of immigration from the Middle East and elsewhere is unsustainable, as Germany's Merkel herself has now found to her chagrin.

As you have seen already, Christians need not concern themselves with the end-time prophecies regarding Jesus in the Quran, since these are more or less a later gnostic version of Christian scriptures initially communicated from a Christian heretic to Mohammad regarding the Second Coming of Jesus Christ.

These heretical beliefs should not matter any more to a Christian than expecting to integrate the Jehovah Witnesses' viewpoint on the Second Coming of Jesus according to the writings of C. T. Russell.

As John told us, there are indeed many antichrists as there have been in the past, but this is not the Antichrist.

*"Dear children, this is the last hour; and as you have heard that the antichrist is coming, even now **many** antichrists have come. This is how we know it is the last hour." **1 John 2:18** (NIV)*

So if the Antichrist is not from the European Union or from the Islamic nations, where is he from ? How will we identify him **before** he comes ? For that answer, we will need to go further back in history, to a meeting that occurred more than 45 years ago. It is there that we will obtain a clue to his identity in the next decade as well as that of the ten horns seen by both the apostle John and the prophet Daniel more than 2000 years ago.

CHAPTER 4
Russia, China and the West

MIKHAIL KALASHNIKOV, THE RUSSIAN DESIGNER OF THE AK-47 assault rifle, reportedly wrote a regretful letter several months before his death asking the head of the Russian Orthodox Church if he was to blame for the deaths of those killed by the guns. The AK-47 has for decades been the world's most popular firearm, favored by guerrillas, terrorists and the soldiers of many armies. An estimated 100 million are spread around the world.

Kalashnikov, told the Russian Patriarch he kept asking himself if he's responsible. "The pain in my soul is unbearable. I keep asking myself the same unsolvable question: If my assault rifle took people's lives that means that I, Mikhail Kalashnikov, ... am responsible for people's deaths," he said in the letter.

The response from the Church was that he had nothing to worry. Mikhail was a true patriot of Russia. "If the weapon is used to defend the Motherland, the Church supports both its creators and the servicemen using it," the Church's spokesman was quoted as saying. The answer also sums up both the Russian as well as the Orthodox Church's ruthlessness towards its enemies.

When Donald John Trump became President of the United States in the most unexpected fashion overnight, conservative Christians heaved a collective sigh of relief. The Russians were the first to cheer, even as the rest of the world including the allies of the US run by socialist leading European governments reacted in dismay. In the capital of Moscow, a campaign was even launched to name a street after Trump following his victory.

However the Russians have always distrusted the United States and the West in general. This feeling is deep-seated and rooted in their history. Why it was and will continue to be this way goes back centuries and even a whole millennium. It is intimately related to the Orthodox Christian faith of the Russians and of Putin.

As recently as 2004, the then Pope of the Catholic church John Paul II delivered a long awaited apology to Orthodox Christians for the Catholic plundering of Constantinople(now Istanbul in Turkey) eight centuries ago in 1204. The sacking of Constantinople, which was part of the Fourth Crusade, was one of the most violent events of the Middle Ages.

The crusading army sacked Constantinople in desperation, having built up a huge debt to the Republic of Venice, which had provided it with ships for the Fourth Crusade against the Muslims in Jerusalem. It contributed to the collapse of the Byzantine Orthodox Empire three centuries later, which was subsequently followed by the Islamization of Asia Minor or what is Turkey today.

Orthodox Christians have never forgiven the Western Catholic church for stabbing them in the back and attempting to destroy them. In fact it took 1000 years to finally arrange a meeting in Cuba between the Catholic and the Orthodox patriarch from Istanbul!

In the 13th century, there were also invasions by the Catholic Teutonic knights from Germany in order to force Russia into the Western Catholic church. This further increased enmity with the Russians who saw the West as increasingly hostile and colonial in nature, attempting to wipe out its own church and traditions and replace them with Western traditions.

The biggest heroes of the Russians commemorated even today are those tsars and princes that stood up to the West. The

Russians in the first few centuries after the first millennium preferred even to pay tribute to the Muslim Tartars(who today make up the central Asian republics) as the price of being allies than be subjugated by the Western Europeans.

Today with the tacit support of the Russian state, many Evangelical and Pentecostal believers are still harshly persecuted in that country and churches declared illegal, shuttered or torn down.

In the political world at large Russia continues this tradition of offense being the best defense. As during the first Korean war of the 1950s, the Soviet Union supported North Korea against the United States, so also today, Russia warns the United States against moving unilaterally against North Korea in its backyard.

In Western nations it clandestinely supports political parties that show some affinity towards Russia, hoping to supplant anti-Russian governments in the West with parties that lean pro-Russian. It also aims to foment chaos in the West as evidenced by efforts both supporting *Trump and anti-Trump* after he won the elections in the United States in November 2016.

Russia has worked to upend the post-Cold War European order through an aggressive campaign of information warfare in recent years so much so that it is now identified as the primary threat to the current order. In 2017, retired Gen. James Mattis, now the U.S. secretary of defense, reiterated that *Russia was the number one threat to the United States* and was engaging in a continuing effort to break the North Atlantic alliance.

Putin declared a decade ago that Russia would execute a foreign policy that no longer recognized a U.S.-led, unipolar system. Putin's stated goal is the restoration of Great Russia. Putin has accused the leaders in the West of treating God and Satan equally. He contrasts the Western secular approach with that of Russia, blaming Western government interference for selling perverted humanist ideals.

Suffice it to say, Russia and the West will not be friendly anytime soon, as long as Russia and Putin cast themselves as both a lone protector of the Christian faith and a powerful counterbalance to Western "hegemony" in the world.

China and the West

Under its leader-for-life Xi, Communist led China is beginning to project massive power from an appetite whetted by its ever increasing population of 1 billion plus. With China's own ambitious OBOR (One Belt One Road) global project, the countries of Europe and the Middle East have also been warming up to the Communist Asian giant.

The earlier occupation of Tibet in 1950 and its ever expanding current games in the South China sea, the Indian ocean and its spanking new military base on the east coast of Africa in the strange sounding Arab Islamic country of Djibouti are only the beginning of what China aims to do, now and in the future.

Not long ago, the political leaders of the Soviet Union railed against the United States and other "imperialist" powers. The Soviet Union then proceeded to crush the East European countries surrounding Russia, undermining the governments in Ukraine, Poland, Lithuania, Romania, Bulgaria, Latvia and others and sending Soviet soldiers to help their communist puppets take over these lands, putting them under the thumb of Moscow.

In 1981 the Soviet Union proceeded to invade Afghanistan ostensibly to prop up the then communist regime of Babrak Karmal in Kabul. The aim of the Soviets was to take their army eventually to the shores of the Indian ocean. The repression of the European and Central Asian peoples behind the Iron Curtain continued till the eventual collapse of the Soviet Union in early 1991.

After the fall of the Soviets, the Chinese saw the writing on the wall for their own equally repressive regime. Built on the

Soviet model, harsh crackdowns on its own citizens came to a head with Mao Zedong and led to the death of 65 million Chinese during the cultural revolution starting in 1966.

The Chinese communist party later under Deng Xiaoping in 1978 relaxed rules of industry encouraging some form of capitalism. They did this while holding firmly onto the reins of power with one party rule that has continued way past the internal citizens' revolt and brutal crackdown on Tianenmen Square in 1989.

In tandem with the Soviets before them, railing against the "imperialist" powers of the West, the Chinese annexed Tibet in 1950 causing the worldwide head of Buddhism, the Dalai Lama to flee to his current sanctuary in India.

China today continues to claim other lands including part of the South China Sea from its many neighbors by building man-made islands and laying claim to new territories beyond its current boundaries.

The Chinese now see the opportunity to go further than the Soviet Union ever did, with their ambitious OBOR project to connect them directly by train or road with countries not previously connected to it in Europe, Asia and even Africa across the Suez Canal.

They want to do this by buying their way into poorer countries along the OBOR by lending money with very high interest rates for badly needed infrastructure in these countries. China has projected itself to have a dominating position in these countries by these unserviceable loans.

Chinese power continues to project exponentially outwards even as the tottering European Union to the West weakens further. In the future Europe will face a greater danger from Russia and China, assuming European countries are able to sensibly manage their own immigration numbers from the Middle East.

With the new US policy of "America First", Trump aims for a calculated withdrawal of the American military from Europe and the Middle East. Unfortunately, America's European and Middle Eastern allies do not appear to be stepping reliably into the gap of overseeing their own defenses against Russia and Iran respectively as Trump would expect.

CHAPTER 5
The Dogs of War

IN 1956, THE ECCENTRIC CHESS GENIUS Bobby Fischer, now widely acclaimed as the greatest grandmaster ever, was only emerging as a great talent, and his results were just good enough to get him an invitation to the Rosenwald Trophy tournament in New York City. Fischer did not have a great tournament there, but at just 13 years old he did play what would become known as The Game of the Century against Donald Byrne.

Fischer made a stunning queen sacrifice early in his game against Byrne. As game enthusiasts will know, the queen piece on the chessboard is the most powerful and it appeared that Bobby was setting up for a game loss. With this well disguised move, he eventually won more than enough lower ranked pieces in exchange before finally checkmating his opponent. The sheer audacity of that game cemented it in history as the greatest ever played.

There is another great game of strategy ongoing for the minds and the souls of men for millennia, but this game is clearly one sided. Satan, the adversary of God and Man, unable to play against God is content to play this game against Man instead, on a giant board of nations, cities and families. His aim is no less than to consign Man to hell along with him and his fallen angels.

He sets one nation against the other, one religious group against the other and exults in the death and destruction that results everywhere, starting from the breakdown of the societal unit of the family to that of entire cities and nations. At this point in time he wants nothing less than a new Western Crusade - Islamic Jihad to occur. But even that is simply the beginning of his plans for us. Jesus Himself tells us:

> *"You will hear of wars and rumors of wars, but see to it that you are not alarmed. Such things must happen, but the end is still to come."* **Mathew 24:6** *(NIV)*

You see, Satan's planned it all in advance. We are dealing with a cunning adversary who once used to be the foremost archangel in God's kingdom before he fell from grace, dragging a third of the angels down with him. This is well known from Isaiah's description of his fall.

> *"The word of the Lord came to me:*
> *"Son of man, take up a lament concerning the king of Tyre and say to him: 'This is what the Sovereign Lord says:*
> *"'You were the seal of perfection,*
> *full of wisdom and perfect in beauty.*
> *13 You were in Eden,*
> *the garden of God;*
> ***every precious stone adorned you:***
> ***carnelian, chrysolite and emerald,***
> ***topaz, onyx and jasper,***
> ***lapis lazuli, turquoise and beryl.***
> ***Your settings and mountings were made of gold;***
> *on the day you were created they were prepared.*
> *14 You were anointed as a guardian cherub,*
> *for so I ordained you.*
> *You were on the holy mount of God;*
> *you walked among the fiery stones.*
> *You were blameless in your ways*

from the day you were created
till wickedness was found in you.
Through your widespread trade
you were filled with violence,
and you sinned.
So I drove you in disgrace from the mount of God,
and I expelled you, guardian cherub,
from among the fiery stones.
Your heart became proud
on account of your beauty,
and you corrupted your wisdom
because of your splendor.
So I threw you to the earth;
*I made a spectacle of you before kings."" **Ezekiel***
***28:11-17** (NIV)*

From the description of Satan in the Bible from Ezekiel's vision, we Christians are aware, even more painfully so than adherents of every other religion on earth of the impossibility of humanly defeating Satan. Satan was once the foremost archangel, the seal of perfection, full of wisdom and perfect in beauty.

As the foremost archangel he was clearly once the angel in charge of worship, as evidenced by the "workmanship of his tabrets(tambourines) and pipes" (Ezekiel 28:13 in the original KJV has "tabrets and pipes" in place of "settings and mountings"). But this position of being second only to the Most Highest made him prideful and seeking that worship for himself, he rebelled and fell from heaven. In that fall, he dragged a third of the angels down with him.

Unmistakingly he therefore is of far higher intelligence than us mortals can hope to possess. We are only aware of Satan's designs for humanity by the inspiration of God to the prophets and our Lord's own recorded life in the Gospels. So we have no excuse for being ignorant of the designs of this supremely malicious enemy, seeing these play out even now among families and nations. We have been warned.

Danger posed to the Abrahamic religions

From the beginnings of Islam, the world has gone through a massively shifting game of empires, mostly between Christianity and Islam for the souls of men. With the decline of Islam along with the European Reformation, the European nations and the New West, notably the United States, Canada and Australia have left their Islamic counterparts in the dust as they undertake newer and massive explorations and mapping of land, sea, air and space.

The Islamic countries have invested a good portion of their new found oil wealth not into nation-building but into fomenting revolution, usually in other Islamic nations, for the spread of their own brand of Islam.

The high stakes game between the formerly Christian nations of the West and the Islamic nations of the Middle East has expectedly ended with the West as insurmountable adversaries. However the spiritual chess-game that started from the garden of Eden is only beginning.

The generation that fought the two world wars is already either gone or passing away. Militarization of individual nation-states is increasing. The world has not yet lost its appetite for carnage and destruction.

The first stage to the adversary's end-game begins with a perceived religious war. It is designed to exponentially accelerate the slow decline of societies loosely based on Abrahamic laws and morals(Christian, Muslim and Jewish) from within.

ISIS and Al-Qaeda are however shadows of their former selves. They are no longer in any significant position to attack the "Dar Al Harb", or the nations of the "unbeliever". These failing movements are no longer sustainable with lone criminal elements, no political power and rapidly disappearing bases and money.

The Queen is gone but the Pawns march on

The world's first globalists according to the book of Genesis were the Babylonians (of the ancient city of Babel), those who under the leadership of the mighty hunter Nimrod aimed even to take over Heaven.

"Then they said, "Come, let us build ourselves a city, with a tower that reaches to the heavens, so that we may make a name for ourselves; otherwise we will be scattered over the face of the whole earth." *Genesis 11:4 (NIV)*

A modern globalist with an abiding hate for God and a similar aim as Nimrod in the past was Karl Marx. Marx writes in his drama "Oulanem", a obvious play on the name Emmanuel: "I'll set up my throne above, Cold and terrible will be the peak of it"

Bukharin, one of Marx's associates, was also an anarchist who hated God. He called Satan the first free thinker and "saviour" of the world, the one who "freed" Adam and impressed the seal of humanity and liberty on his forehead, by making him disobedient.

To the Christian conservative today it appears Satanic "Babylonian" style globalism is on the retreat everywhere as nationalistic patriotic parties take over the United States and parts of East Europe and even Russia. There is a lot to cheer for as human beings reject elite globalist ideas and international socialism, the continually failing poster child of obsolete communism and Marxism.

The queen of Globalism appears to be dead, but the pawns are still grouping for a counter attack employing the mainstream news and social media of the progressive elite.

Today's politicians in parts of the West are once again increasingly swayed by spiritual advisers who see the Islamic nations as a thorn in the side of Israel against the rebuilding of the third Jewish temple. So there is an eager awaiting of the final war in some quarters to facilitate the removal of the current Al-Aqsa mosque and allow this rebuilding of the third temple at Jerusalem so the Messiah can return.

In the midst of this believing and wise Christians should never forget that Christ blessed the peacemakers(**Matthew 5:9**). He never blessed any warmongers ! Sure, we know America has to deal with deception from some Muslim nation every now and then. We also know the concept of taqqiyah(allowed denial of Islamic belief when required) can be used to further the aims of political Islam.

But even moderate Muslim nations such as Jordan and Egypt that have made long lasting peace with Israel today no longer see America as a honest broker in the Middle East between the Israeli Jews and the Muslim nations. Into this powder-keg of high emotions, where will the rising dragon China and the Christian yet staunchly anti-West Russia enter?

The answer to that question will bring us to the start of World War 3 that will eventually devastate and destroy most nations. A devastating world war will take out all existing power structures we see today and inevitably bring down Western and Middle Eastern governments that run, loosely today on constitutions based on their own interpretations of Abrahamic and the Mosaic moral laws.

The implications of such a worldwide war will be especially staggering to the religious conservative. But as the Lord states in **Mathew 24:6** above, its not the end. But it is definitely a prelude to the final kingdom of Man that will follow.

It is for those of the Abrahamic religions that consider Abraham as their spiritual father - namely the Christians,

Muslims and Jews to let cooler minds prevail in the West, the Middle East and Israel so that this war does not engulf the entire world, no matter how they perceive each other at present.

However as can be seen with Shiite Iran baiting the west and with a few apocalypse infatuated Christians having the ear of America's politicians, there is a possibility that the situation will spill over into war in the future.

It is quite likely that Trump being the consummate businessman that he is, more dedicated to the continuing prosperity of the United States and fellow Americans will not make the first move.

He has shown an uncanny ability to play good cop, bad cop while keeping the pressure on America's current enemies, taking them out from within, rather than without. This has actually been possible with Iran's nuclear ambitions in the past with the setting back of its nuclear program by the clever use of cyber warfare.

And hopefully America's current enemies will continue to have trouble reading his real intentions, staying in the current impasse. However Iran and the unstable regime in North Korea facing a revolt from its own starving citizenry and soldiers under increasing sanctions is still the powder keg that go off at any moment, predictably in Trump's second term in office from 2020-2024.

War is pretty much inevitable, in the near future. The Jewish prophets Isaiah, Ezekiel, Daniel, Zechariah and others have already seen this war of the future. Our Lord however tells us that war **is not the end** of tribulations as in Mathew 24:6. There is more.

CHAPTER 6
Enter the dragon

JESUS SPOKE OF THE TIMES OF THE GENTILES after the destruction of Israel and the forced diaspora of the Jews by the Roman empire out of Israel into the territories of the Roman empire. When the times of the Gentiles are fulfilled with the creation of Israel again in 1948, He then talks about the signs of global climate change, increased earthquakes and rising sea levels that will terrify the earth's inhabitants.

"They will fall by the sword and will be taken as prisoners to all the nations. Jerusalem will be trampled on by the Gentiles until the times of the Gentiles are fulfilled. There will be signs in the sun, moon and stars. On the earth, nations will be in anguish and perplexity at the roaring and tossing of the sea." **Luke 21:24** *(NIV)*

These climate signs also take place as the world is preparing for war and nation is rising against nation. In additions He also tells us of famines and worldwide epidemics at this time.

"Nation will rise against nation, and kingdom against kingdom. There will be famines and earthquakes in various places." **Matthew 24:7** *(NIV)*

There is little doubt that those times are now creeping up on us. Like the birth pangs of soon-to-be new mother of a baby, the frequency and magnitude of these earth shaking events will increase with time. The mainstream media too strives to inform us today of this terrifying climate change that they and their elite progressive leaders blame solely on humanity's misuse of the earth's resources.

Most Christians are by now aware that we are living in that time that Jesus spoke of. To understand that this is no coincidence you only need to go to the events on December 26, 2003 and December 26, 2004 a year later. On the day after Christmas in 2003, Iran experienced a devastating earthquake in Bam with a magnitude of 6.6 for a whole of 12 seconds that took 26,271 lives damaging or destroying 90% of the buildings in that city. Exactly a year later, the day after Christmas 2004, the most devastating earthquake in the modern history of planet Earth took place. Starting as a magnitude 9.3 earthquake that shook the earth for a shocking 10 minutes starting in the Indian Ocean, the earthquake spawned a 98 foot tsunami traveling a full 8 hours across the Indian ocean hitting several nations in Asia and Africa and led to the loss of 230,000 lives including over 1000 Westerners.

Frightening in its magnitude and global reach the entire world felt its repercussions. Sweden that had not suffered such a massive loss of citizenry in a single event since 1709 had a minor parliamentary crisis on account of the handling of the tsunami thousands of miles away. A similarly huge quake shook Japan in March 2011, spawned a tsunami, moved the west coast of that country 8 feet and shifted the axis of Earth 4 inches, while shortening the Earth day for all of us.

In a similar way to the increasing pains of an expectant mother, as in the earth's shakings and violent natural events on land and sea, political tensions are also increasing worldwide in both frequency and strength. Indeed the mother of all human wars is building up on the near horizon.

World War 3 and the alliance against Israel

John in the book of Revelation(Apocalypse) talks of a massive world war that leads to the death of one third of the world's population. The war is started when four fallen angels bound(Jude 1:6) at the Euphrates river are released. Note that the Euphrates river though associated with Iraq actually originates in *eastern Turkey* flowing into both Syria and Iraq and finally ending in the Persian Gulf at the border of Iraq and Iran.

The sixth angel sounded his trumpet, and I heard a voice coming from the four horns of the golden altar that is before God. It said to the sixth angel who had the trumpet, "Release the four angels who are bound at the great river Euphrates. And the four angels who had been kept ready for this very hour and day and month and year were released to kill a third of mankind."
Revelation 9:13-15 *(NIV)*

The future alliance coming against Israel is also clearly mentioned by several Bible prophets. These include Ezekiel, Daniel, Zechariah and others. John then corroborates what these prophets of old have already told us, that a future mother of all world wars will originate in the Middle East(something that is yet to happen). Today this can be clearly linked to Shiite Muslim ascendancy and a likely *nominal* Sunni ally such as Turkey in that region of the Middle East.

Interestingly after the fall of Saddam Hussein's strictly Sunni Muslim regime, Iraq is now firmly in the hand of its majority Shiites for the first time *since 1932* and is readily doing the bidding of Iran's government while purporting to side with the United States. This corroboration by John more than 600 years after Ezekiel is stunning in its prophetic and political synchronization today. Neither John nor Ezekiel would have known how what they saw would actually happen. But it is clear to us in this generation.

*"Son of man, set your face against Gog, of the land of Magog, the chief prince of Meshek and Tubal; prophesy against him and say: 'This is what the Sovereign Lord says: I am against you, Gog, chief prince of Meshek and Tubal. I will turn you around, put hooks in your jaws and bring you out with your whole army--your horses, your horsemen fully armed, and a great horde with large and small shields, all of them brandishing their swords. Persia, Cush and Put will be with them, all with shields and helmets, also Gomer with all its troops, and Beth Togarmah from the far north with all its troops--the many nations with you." **Ezekiel 38:2-6** (NIV)*

Meshek and Tubal that comprised Asia Minor or Anatolia in the ancient maps lay beside Greece and are perceived to be modern day Turkey, still the long sworn enemy of Greece. Gog may therefore refer to the Turkish leader. However Gog is NOT the Antichrist. If he was, John would have mentioned Gog instead of 666 in Revelation 13. John knew the Hebrew scriptures, having understood them even more deeply at the foot of Christ. There would no need for John to provide the Antichrist's name so seemingly cryptically.

Another reason we know that Gog is not the Antichrist is because the Antichrist appears to be thrown down directly into hell by Jesus while Gog dies in Israel. There is no mention of Gog encountering his death at the Second Coming of Jesus. Notice the clear differences between these two verses regarding the fate of Gog and Antichrist from Ezekiel and the book of Revelation by St John. Gog also has no false prophet beside him. If it was a false prophet egging the Turkish leader on, then this same false prophet is unlikely to deceive Christians into following him as mentioned in the book of Revelation. Just reflect on how ridiculous that sounds in the first place.

If you compare and contrast Gog in the prophecies of Ezekiel and the Beast of Antichrist in the Book of Revelation, you will see clear differences in the way they meet their ends.

"Son of man, prophesy against Gog and say: 'This is what the Sovereign Lord says: I am against you, Gog, chief prince of

Meshek and Tubal. I will turn you around and drag you along. I will bring you from the far north and send you against the mountains of Israel. Then I will strike your bow from your left hand and make your arrows drop from your right hand. On the mountains of Israel you will fall, you and all your troops and the nations with you. I will give you as food to all kinds of carrion birds and to the wild animals. You will fall in the open field, for I have spoken, declares the Sovereign Lord. I will send fire on Magog and on those who live in safety in the coastlands, and they will know that I am the Lord." **Ezekiel 39:1-6** *(NIV)*

"And the beast was seized, and with him the false prophet who performed the signs in his presence, by which he deceived those who had received the mark of the beast and those who worshiped his image; these two were thrown alive into the lake of fire which burns with brimstone." **Revelation 19:20** *(NASB)*

The fates of the two are clearly very different. We don't see Gog or Magog mentioned anywhere for this particular time by the apostle John (John does however clearly reuse the term "Gog and Magog" to denote the ends of the earth after a thousand years of peace, at a later time in **Revelation 20:7-9**). The Antichrist comes after many wars well after Gog has already been killed on the battlefield in Israel. In fact there appears to be no relation between the two at all - they belong to two different times but as you will see later, not really that far apart.

Yet the antichrist Gog of many known antichrists throughout history is simply a pawn in the endgame of Satan who will animate and send out the final Antichrist in his wake. There are many antichrists already throughout history including many false prophets and leaders - we are also interested in the Antichrist with a capital "A" - the final one mentioned described by the apostle John.

Now we will turn to the other countries in the alliance against Israel. Persia is of course Iran, sometimes still used in some places to refer to the Iranians. Cush is Sudan that lies below Egypt and is also fed by the same Nile river. How do we know this? In Nahum 3, this is clear from the Lord's mocking of the proud city of Nineveh:

> *"Are you better than Thebes,*
> *situated on the Nile,*
> *with water around her?*
> *The river was her defense,*
> *the waters her wall.*
> *Cush and Egypt were her boundless strength;*
> *Put and Libya were among her allies."* **Nahum 3:8-9**
> *(NIV)*

Similarly, from the above verse, the country below Libya - namely Chad and even possibly the other countries west and north of it in N. Africa is called Put or Phut. These are also Islamic nations - all of them. Cush and Phut were sons of Ham, son of Noah. Biblical scholars have placed them as the ancestors of the African tribes.

Beth Togarmah or House of Togarmah refers to the Turkic or Turkmen tribes that spread out across from eastern Anatolia (Turkey) to the east and the north to what is present day Turkmenistan, Azerbaijan and other countries of Central Asia that formed part of the ex-Soviet republics along with Russia two decades ago. These are also majority Islamic nations except for Armenia.

You will notice that among all those nations in the alliance against Israel above - one prominently mentioned in the Bible in other places is missing in the alliance - Kedar or Dedan - the place of the Arab tribes, represented chiefly by Saudi Arabia among the Arab sheikhdoms of the Middle East, the seat of Sunni Islam. Another prominent kingdom is also missing, further underscored in Daniel 11. It is the Hashemite kingdom of Jordan to the immediate east of Israel that incidentally shares Israel's longest border with any country! (Shiite ruled Syria lies to the North-east of Israel and shares a tinier border with Israel - the Golan Heights). Edom, Moab and Ammon in ancient times now collectively form modern-day south and north Jordan

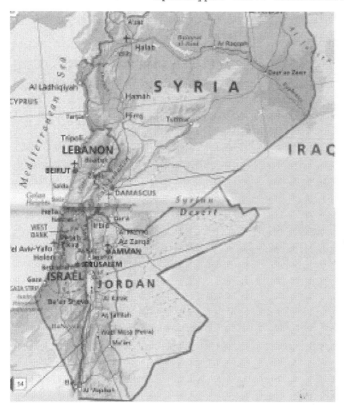

The end-time prophecies of Daniel 11 start from Daniel 11:40. For the sake of brevity, we will simply remember from other historical and other scholarly sources that the first half of Daniel 11 refer to prophecies that were fulfilled 200 years after Daniel.

The pre-endtime Daniel 11:36-39 verses deal with the Hellenistic Syrian king Antiochus Epiphanes (214-165 BC) who desolated the Jewish temple and attempted to force Hellenistic customs on the Jews. Antiochus Epiphanes was then opposed by the Jewish Maccabees.

We will not go further into details of how the Hellenistic Syrian king Antiochus Epiphanes fulfills **Daniel 11:37-38** as he did not respect Tammuz the god of fertility, the god that women loved(*Ezekiel 8:14*) or how he honored only the supreme Greek "god" Zeus Akraios, the god of the fortresses (1¹). Antiochus even forced the Jews on pain of death to accept these in the Jewish temple in Jerusalem, sacrificing a pig to Zeus, thus causing an "abomination of desolation" and triggering the Jewish rebellion by the Maccabees.

The "abomination of desolation" then re-occurs in history again following this initial desolation by Antiochus, as foretold by Jesus with the Romans destroying the second temple of Solomon in 70 AD. In addition there is a future abomination established in the Jewish temple by the Antichrist himself.

It may be possible that the *Daniel 11:37-38* verses have a second fulfillment in the future - that the Antichrist will also honor the god of fortresses or ignore the god of women, though it is not clear what role those minor gods have today, so it seems more unlikely that Tammuz and Zeus Akraios will make a comeback in the future. Certainly we are not ruling it out - but Antiochus Epiphanes has already fulfilled this verse once in a more ancient age.

The four horns or kingdoms seen by Daniel but not later by John

The same principle applies in *Daniel 8* too relating to the four horns. The ram and the goat in Daniel 8 have already been explained by the angel in *Daniel 8:20 and 8:21* - named as Medo-Persia and Greece. After Alexander the Great's(the goat) conquest of the known world in 12 short years and his untimely death, four kingdoms emerged from the breakup in the West, East, North and South - Egypt-Northeast Africa (Ptolemaic), Iraq-Iran (Seleucid), Macedonia-Greece (Cassandrian) and Turkey-Asia Minor (Lysimachean) named after his four generals Ptolemy, Seleucus, Cassander and Lysimachus.

All this is then fulfilled prophecy but for the little horn seen by Daniel in the future and the ten horns(again with the little horn) also seen by John 300 years later. John does not see the ram and the goat or the four generals and their four kingdoms all gone by mid 200 BC, well before John is born but he sees only ten horns just as Daniel sees in his end times visions.

So we know that Daniel himself refers to the end time prophecies regarding World War 3 starting at the 11:40 verses. So rather than debate on Daniel 11:37-38 or Daniel 8 regarding the four horns and *forcibly* fit Gog to those once again, we will primarily concern ourselves with the 11:40 verses onward.

"At the time of the end the king of the South will engage him in battle, and the king of the North will storm out against him with chariots and cavalry and a great fleet of ships. He will invade many countries and sweep through them like a flood. He will also invade the Beautiful Land. Many countries will fall, but Edom, Moab and the leaders of Ammon will be delivered from his hand. He will extend his power over many countries; Egypt will not escape." **Daniel 11:40-42** *(NIV)*

Edom, Moab and Ammon as we have seen collectively refer to Jordan, which with Saudi Arabia is an ally of the United States and has a peace treaty of its own with Israel since 1994!

Again in Ezekiel 38, Sheba and Dedan are mentioned as standing afar and watching the war unfold under Gog, the leader of Turkey and his alliance against Israel. Sheba and Dedan are the lands of Arabia allied with Tarshish, that is the islands across the sea from Israel, a reference to the sea traders of Europe. This is also a time when Israel is living securely.

"Sheba and Dedan and the merchants of Tarshish with all its villages will say to you, 'Have you come to capture spoil? Have you assembled your company to seize plunder, to carry away silver and gold, to take away cattle and goods, to capture great spoil?' Therefore prophesy, son of man, and say to Gog, 'Thus says the Lord God, "On that day when My people Israel are living securely, will you not know it?"'" **Ezekiel 38:13 (NASB)**

The diligent student of eschatology may ask about the aforementioned regions of Jordan being devastated in Psalm 83. Psalm 83 mentions the Sunni nations that include Jordan, parts of Iraq and the others but again interestingly omit Iran that comes up against the Jewish people. The significance of this Psalm will be clear in a later chapter of this book. This Psalm refers to a later time.

The now established absence of the most zealous Arab Sunni nations in this war is as expected. For this is an alliance of only the Shia Muslims represented by Iran and Syria's current leaders and those nominal Sunnis that align with them(Turkey) that is coming against Israel and its ally, the United States. Most of the Sunnis stand aside, except a few nominally Sunni nations among the Central Asian republics and Lebanon that are not inimical to Iran.

Lebanon itself is equally split between Sunni, Shiite and Christian with the Hezbollah having previously turned the tide towards Shiite ascendancy in that country. These "absent" Sunni nations prefer to wait and watch from the sidelines as they hope that their Shia enemies will be destroyed first and perhaps after that with a little more luck Israel too, in that order.

Saudi Arabia however is still bothered by Yemenite forces under the control of Iran in the south. Iran is more interested in the destruction of Israel. Saudi Arabia is content to watch and wait. For Saudi Arabia would prefer any day to be an ally of Jewish Israel than accept the Shiites of Iran or ally with them. To Saudi Arabia that(Shiiteism) would be the greater anathema.

The Setup to World War 3 - why the next four years are crucial

CAUTION: The rest of this will be informed political speculation but a reader of today's news can see where this is all heading. Eventually the weakening EU will be unable to resist its growing and unmanageable financial problems as it breaks apart into separate nation states and the economic power of the central government in Brussels weakens. Germany will fail to hold the EU together under the onslaught of unsustainable immigration and failing economies of the southern European nations.

China makes inroads into East Europe with its OBOR project together with Russia as the United States disengages slowly from Europe and the Middle East. Egypt and North African countries accept Chinese handling of the Suez port in return for investment in their economy. The Arab impoverished country of Djibouti on Africa's east coast is already in debt to China for its huge investment there. The United States slowly withdraws its troops from the Middle East, trusting powerful Israel and their Arab Sunni allies to be able to hold off their internal and external enemies without US help. A great economy and all round prosperity propels Trump to power for another 4 years in 2020.

However in early 2021, the world economy is getting overheated and running out of steam. Inflation is out of control and the stock market value of companies grossly overpriced to actual earnings. There are rumblings in economies in Asia and Europe and increased hits to the economies of Asia, Europe and the United States not just from trade wars but also from increasing natural disasters - earthquakes, hurricanes and longer wintry conditions that turn harsher especially in the West. *These increase in line with the prophecies of Jesus Christ before His second coming.*

North Korea's increasingly erratic ruler finally decides to flex his nuclear muscle as Trump gets re-elected in 2020 to the Presidentship of the United States. In 2020-21, weakened by kidney disease and end-stage dialysis, Kim Jong Un aims to make an example of Japan, (not South Korea that it prefers for land conquest and eventual unification of the Koreas). This attack on Japan might serve as an "advance warning" to the United States.

China refuses to accept proof of North Korean complicity and supports North Korea, complementing an initially low profile war over land with the United States and Japan. Russia pledges help to North Korea but does not directly enter the war yet preferring to watch from the sidelines offering Russian weaponry and planes to North Korea and China.

Increasingly synchronous actions of Tehran with Pyongyang - News from the North and the East

On July 27th, 2017 Iran test launched a rocket of its own into space. The very next day, North Korea tested a ballistic missile that overflew Japan and ended in the sea just beyond it. While to the most of the world the timing of the two events appeared to be just a coincidence, it is widely believed that the events were synchronized to catch the United States off guard.

It is widely known among international intelligence that Iranian and North Korean scientists routinely meet and exchange information on ballistic and nuclear weapons technology that North Korea possesses. Iranian scientists under disguised names travel to North Korea via Beijing to observe the routine atomic weapons detonation by that country. North Korea's signature has been found on chemical weapons used by the Syrian government that are received via Iran and transported across the border via Iraq to Damascus.

At the time of speaking the Iranian government has brought and paid for tens of thousands of Shiite Muslim mercenaries with Iranian money now released by the previous US administration. They also employ some of this money to pay Lebanese Hezbollah and Syrian Shiite fighters to establish bases across the border from Israel, readying themselves for a future onslaught in a time of their choice. Iran is also front-loading Syria's villages bordering Israel with Shiites it helps transport from Shia villages in Iraq and Lebanon.

However it also does not help that the current Iranian regime, made up of Twelvers, similar to the Sunni terrorist group ISIS before it, has an apocalyptic vision in which their Mahdi cannot arrive until there is chaos in the world. And so it is why Iran aim to foment chaos in the Middle East, in Yemen and

Lebanon and Syria, whenever and wherever they can.

Today the Iranian government is not only facing widespread anger from the Arab Sunnis and their governments in the Middle East but recently even faced an internal revolt of its own making. Angry Iranians took to the streets to demand why they had seen no money flow to them from the $150 billion that was promised by the previous US administration in return for international checks on their nuclear material. Instead that money has flowed to the Iranian government's proxies in Lebanon and Syria.

The synchronicity of events between the North Korean military and the Iranians is expected to increase. Events will come to a head when the situation on the Korean peninsula turns into active war as Iran sees its chance to create a second front to attack Israel and ensure the weakened participation of the United States, the nuclear war situation on the Korean peninsula being far more dangerous. To this end it may acquire or may have already acquired nuclear bombs from North Korea if it has not already developed a nuclear weapons capacity by 2020-21.

Changing geopolitical realities in the world as America withdraws

Ruling leftist parties in South and Latin America in solidarity against "Western and Zionist imperialism" allow Islamic radicals free passage in their nations supporting the Iranian cause against "apartheid" Israel. This is a follow-up from earlier having accepted Chinese and Iranian money to prop up their weakening economies under socialist rule. Mexican and Canadian drug gangs co-operate with Shiite Islamic radicals in infiltrating the US while Mexico's socialist government looks the other way. South American countries already have Chinese military bases in return for Chinese investment in their economies.

World War 3 wreaks havoc across the world with strategically placed targeted nuclear attacks. Since Russia, China and the United States are mindful of mutually assured destruction, their attacks using these weapons are calculated and not all out against the other.

Finally the seemingly endless stalemate comes to an end in 2024, when Russia grows increasingly distrustful of China's intentions and it finally switches over to the Western alliance, turning the tide of the war. Iranian, Syrian, Lebanese, Turkish and North African Muslim troops march towards Israel determined to finish off the Israelis. Israel retaliates with nukes with US help. Its Iron Dome system cannot stop all missiles. Some parts of Israel are made desolate during the war.

The end of World War 3

World War 3 finally comes to an end as Russia switches sides. How this will exactly happen is not clear. It is also why Russia is not formally mentioned in the alliance against Israel. The word "Rosh", for example as used in the well known Jewish feast of Rosh Hashanah or the "Head of the year" feast refers to "chief" or "head". Thus Rosh refers to the head of the alliance against Israel and not specifically to the country of Russia. This is its exact meaning in the Bible where the word "Rosh" appears no less than 600 times !

Yet where Russia sits at any time, is where the victory in this war shifts. Falling out with China, Russia consolidates its gains and supports the Western alliance as the Soviets did with the US and Britain at the end of World War 2 in the last century and Russia and America did with ISIS a decade earlier. Embattled and losing morale to continue the devastating war, China requests an armistice but without conditions. The equally weakened forces of the Western alliance agree and war comes to an end in the first half of 2024.

The war weary world and the media blame conservatives in their countries for war mongering, with the mainstream and social media heavily influencing the progressive perspective of the war. The new progressive governments in the West enforce peace without conditions. Trump gets ready to leave office in late 2024 and in Russia, Putin finally comes to the end of the last of his 24 years in office also in 2024 after his final 6 years are up.

Worldwide depression is slowly winding up with the last war. Both leaders leave power vacuums that are filled up by progressive front-runners after the world-wide disgust for the last nuclear world war and overwhelming desire for world peace. Yet more treachery is afoot. Isaiah has given us a verse for this time when the final devastation is finished.

"From the ends of the earth we hear songs, "Glory to the Righteous One,"
But I say, "Woe to me! Woe to me! Alas for me!
The treacherous deal treacherously,
*And the treacherous deal very treacherously." **Isaiah 24:16** (NASB)*

The inevitability of immoral progressive governments taking over worldwide after this devastating war will next become clear in the following chapters. The prophet Isaiah himself saw this happening, especially in Israel before the time of the Lord's Second Coming. Once again John corroborates humanity's overwhelming lack of remorse or repentance, turning their backs to God even after a devastating war in which one third of the world's population is wiped out and other plagues.

"The rest of mankind who were not killed by these plagues still did not repent of the work of their hands; they did not stop worshiping demons, and idols of gold, silver, bronze, stone and wood--idols that cannot see or hear or walk. Nor did they repent of their murders, their magic arts, their sexual immorality or

*their thefts." **Revelation 9:20-21** (NIV)*

CHAPTER 7
Political earthquakes in 2024

THE PROPHET ISAIAH TALKS OF A CURSE that devours the earth before the Lord's Coming. Additionally there is a strange verse in which seven apparently self-sufficient even well-off single women approach 1 man in order to be married and bear his name.

> *"Therefore a curse consumes the earth;*
>   *its people must bear their guilt.*
> *Therefore earth's inhabitants are burned up,*
>   *and very few are left."* **Isaiah 24:6 (NIV)**

> *"In that day seven women*
>   *will take hold of one man*
> *and say, "We will eat our own food*
>   *and provide our own clothes;*
> *only let us be called by your name.*
>   *Take away our disgrace!"'"* **Isaiah 4:1 (NIV)**

The above verses might seem strange except by now in the immediate aftermath of World War 3 it will be entirely possible. The Bible always turns out to be correct on these future events even if we did not understand earlier how this would happen. And very literally so.

Again in Isaiah 3, the end-times in Israel are described in which it is ruled by a progressive female leader and its officials are young inexperienced youth and when sins are paraded openly in the streets. What does it all mean ? When is this happening ? Here Isaiah 3:4-12 and the description of the youth seems eerily reminiscent of millennial youth even in the West today.

> *"And I will give children to be their princes,*
> *and babes shall rule over them.*
> *And the people shall be oppressed,*
> *every one by another, and every one by his neighbour:*
> *the child shall behave himself proudly against the ancient,*
> *and the base against the honourable." **Isaiah 3:4-5** (NIV)*

Isaiah refers to immature youth oppressing the honorable elders of Israel and (in today's terms) progressive rebellious women ruling over them.

> *"For Jerusalem is ruined, and Judah is fallen:*
> *because their tongue and their doings are against the Lord,*
> *to provoke the eyes of his glory.*
> *The shew of their countenance doth witness against them;*
> *and they declare their sin as Sodom, they hide it not.*
> *Woe unto their soul! for they have rewarded evil unto*
> themselves.
> *Say ye to the righteous, that it shall be well with him:*
> *for they shall eat the fruit of their doings.*
> *Woe unto the wicked! it shall be ill with him:*
> *for the reward of his hands shall be given him.*
> *As for my people, children are their oppressors,*
> *and women rule over them.*
> *O my people, they which lead thee cause thee to err,*
> *and destroy the way of thy paths." **Isaiah 3:8-12** (NIV)*

Israel has already had a highly respected conservative

female prime minister in the late 1960s but clearly that is not the times mentioned here. Golda Meir a self-proclaimed "weary" woman took over the Israeli Government as prime minister after the death in office of Levi Eshkol and quickly retired in early 1974 after the 1973 Yom Kippur war. A future female progressive leader in Israel will force Israel under the leadership of Antichrist to make peace with the Arabs. How that will happen is also elaborated below, with help from her Arab sisters in leadership in the Middle East who reach out to her after World War III. The Antichrist will then make peace between the Jew and the Arab, a peace that will end with treachery and backstabbing after the walls have finally come down.

Though Isaiah has written this (Isaiah 4:1) verse primarily about Israel in the last days after the devastation of the war against it, it is easier to understand that along with the decimation in Israel's fighting men, there is a corresponding decimation in men the world over that make up the armies that engage for and against Israel. After all, Israeli men are not fighting women from other nations! Neither are henpecked Israeli men committing mass suicide. So it is extremely easy to extrapolate this to a worldwide reduction of men through a global war that ends in Israel. Isaiah is clear on this skewed gender ratio and it can be implied that there is a corresponding reflection of the same in the non-Jewish countries after the war.

The consequences of this devastation on the world are devastating both economically and politically. A question arises - we've had two world wars - so why didn't these predictions on lasting peace under progressive leadership come true earlier ? For one thing America was still religiously conservative till the 1960s, and so was most of the world. The internet was not invented yet and there were no massive echo-chambers on social media or Twitter to organize by gender or political affinity on such a wide scale as we have today. Women at the time mostly voted with their husbands.

After a devastating World War 3, many women will revolt against the war and attempt to install their sisters in leadership positions to prevent angry men from ever starting another nuclear war again, just as even today some women overwhelmingly organize for a progressive female leader in the US. Democracy with one adult guaranteed one vote will help progressive women to gain power and make peace between their countries, under the leadership of Antichrist, who will be a man they idolize. However this will not help them in the Middle East or Africa where female voting is restricted, at least at the beginning.

The absolutely inevitable prediction at this point is that we will see finally a female progressive President of the United States when Trump leaves in 2024. After Putin also finally leaves office in 2024, there is a high likelihood that a progressive leader will take over in Russia. And this is how it will happen.

After the devastation of the last world war, with the sex ratio flipping in favor of females (2^2)women voters hold absolute power in the 2024 elections in the United States and Russia and vote for overwhelmingly female progressive anti-war candidates. The government bureaucrats, artistic celebrities and rich technocrats create a world advisory council to prevent all future wars from happening. The world will then finally have a true "United Nations" and a global citizenship to offer each person on the planet.

Governments undergo a sea change everywhere from US to Israel to Poland and Russia as conservative governments are voted out. Progressive parties win in these nations in landslides, largely helped by the decimation in the male population during the war and a large number of female candidates that are nominated and elected for leadership in these countries. The world will finally appear be at peace. But the final deception of humanity is soon to materialize, from the ashes of World War 3.

In fact without this final deception and falling away of the rest of humanity toward all manner of evil, we are told that Jesus will not yet come to save the remnant of those who believe in Him.

"Let no one in any way deceive you, for it will not come unless the apostasy comes first, and the man of lawlessness is revealed, the son of destruction, who opposes and exalts himself above every so-called god or object of worship, so that he takes his seat in the temple of God, displaying himself as being God." **2 Thessalonians 2:3-4** *(NASB)*

CHAPTER 8
A new agenda and a new age

THE APOSTLE JOHN might appear in the Book of Revelation to give us a cryptic puzzle to solve on the final kingdom of the Beast or Antichrist, except that he himself literally saw this materialize as a leadership hierarchy of the Antichrist and 10 other contemporary "kings" under him, not as kings following each other.

> *"Here is the mind which has wisdom. The seven heads are seven mountains on which the woman sits, and they are seven kings; five have fallen, one is, the other has not yet come; and when he comes, he must remain a little while. The beast which was and is not, is himself also an eighth and is one of the seven, and he goes to destruction. The ten horns which you saw are ten kings who have not yet received a kingdom, but they receive authority as kings with the beast for one hour. These have one purpose, and they give their power and authority to the beast."* **Revelation 17:9-13** *(NASB)*

Five centuries before him the prophet Daniel saw the exact same thing.

> *"After this I kept looking in the night visions, and behold, a fourth beast, dreadful and terrifying and extremely strong; and it had large iron teeth. It devoured and crushed and trampled*

down the remainder with its feet; and it was different from all the beasts that were before it, and it had ten horns. While I was contemplating the horns, behold, another horn, a little one, came up among them, and three of the first horns were pulled out by the roots before it; and behold, this horn possessed eyes like the eyes of a man and a mouth uttering great boasts." **Daniel 7:7-8** *(NASB)*

In fact the prophecies of Daniel and the apostle John agree perfectly with each other. There are also many clues above as to the ten horns of the Antichrist. The Beast is like no God-created animal on earth that Daniel has ever seen (unlike the first three) and for this reason it is all the more terrifying to behold.

"Then I desired to know the exact meaning of the fourth beast, which was different from all the others, exceedingly dreadful, with its teeth of iron and its claws of bronze, and which devoured, crushed and trampled down the remainder with its feet, and the meaning of the ten horns that were on its head and the other horn which came up, and before which three of them fell, namely, that horn which had eyes and a mouth uttering great boasts and which was larger in appearance than its associates. I kept looking, and that horn was waging war with the saints and overpowering them until the Ancient of Days came and judgment was passed in favor of the saints of the Highest One, and the time arrived when the saints took possession of the kingdom.

"Thus he said: 'The fourth beast will be a fourth kingdom on the earth, which will be different from all the other kingdoms and will devour the whole earth and tread it down and crush it. As for the ten horns, out of this kingdom ten kings will arise; and another will arise after them, and he will be different from the previous ones and will subdue three kings. He will speak out

*against the Most High and wear down the saints of the Highest One, and he will intend to make alterations in times and in law; and they will be given into his hand for a time, times, and half a time." **Daniel 7:19-25** (NASB)*

In addition Daniel gives additional clues regarding the horns, talking about the overthrow of three of the ten horns, which is explained in later chapters of this book. The Antichrist gives credence to the ten horns as they would not exist without him or his structure. Therefore the ten horns are the ten kings or overseers of ten regions that the entire world is divided into.

The interesting point about the fourth beast that Daniel mentions - that it is different from all the other beasts and he has seen nothing like it before, and so he cannot describe it as he does the first three beasts as having characteristics of known animals. It will be clearer why he is unable to describe this fourth creature in a later chapter where the Antichrist is identified, for it is not an animal that humanity has seen before. It signifies and is intimately linked to the nature of the Antichrist.

A new united government for the world is proposed

How the unified world government will come about is not a new idea to everyone alive even today. It has been proposed earlier, in fact exactly 45 years ago. The document under which these 10 regions was first covered was a report called "Regionalized and Adaptive Model of the Global World System" from the global think tank called Club of Rome. After World War 3, the progressive agenda in this report will be revived as quickly as it was dismissed earlier to prevent the world from ever going to war again. In fact as the Antichrist is aware he needs to move quickly given only 3.5 years or 1260 days to turn the whole world to him. How the world government follows from past history is detailed below.

After World War 3, the United Nations is officially dissolved as a historically impotent player on the world stage. Too weary to resist after the devastating war, regional councils take over with backing from progressive parties to oversee the functioning of the dilapidated nation states. Ten regions are proposed with ten overseers as seen by the Apostle John in the Book of Revelation. These regions with their overseers are the ten horns of the Antichrist, who is the little horn and gives them this temporal power under him.

"The ten horns which you saw are ten kings who have not yet received a kingdom, but they receive authority as kings with the beast for one hour." **Revelation 17:12** *(NASB)*

Technocrats including the CEOs of social media and internet administration companies ensure that all conservative opinion is squelched and appropriately penalized and removed from their domains. Any internet site even vaguely injurious or hateful to the progressive cause is disconnected from their domain servers and unreachable. It is the dictatorship of the remnant and news is now tightly controlled. It is no longer the news that matters but in the words of a mainstream news editor today, the "perception" of that news to the potential voter.

In a world overrun by virtual reality both by instantaneous digital manipulation of what we see and hear in the news, the perception of the news is also easily tailored on the social media cloud and immediately viewable on our mobile devices.

A progressive female party leader is elected president of the United States in 2024 and also in 2024 Russia possibly also has a new female or progressive President after Putin. Female leaders sweep Europe as now women in majority become the main movers and shakers in politics and take a stand against war. Overwhelmingly progressive women are voted into power everywhere.

A worldwide union is now readily implemented on the lines of the Club of Rome's (or more likely the newer and more influential Club of Madrid) recommendation in September 1973. The final union may or may not be the same as in their proposal, but both the apostle John and the prophet Daniel saw the world union of ten kingdoms much like this, run by a single individual at the top.

And what is the Club of Rome ? The Club of Rome describes itself as an organization of individuals (not based in Rome at this time) who share a common concern for the future of humanity and strive to make a difference. Their mission ostensibly is to promote understanding of the global challenges facing humanity and to propose solutions.

Founded in 1968 in Rome, Italy, the CoR consists of current and former heads of state, scientists including those from MIT here in the United States, economists and business leaders from around the globe. It gained considerable public attention in 1972 with its first report, "The Limits to Growth". The report sold 30 million copies in more than 30 languages, becoming the best-selling environmental book in history.

Since 1 July 2008 the organization has been based in Winterthur, Switzerland. This is not to say that the CoR in Switzerland makes up the world government during the time of the Antichrist, but the point being that several influential political figures have already theorized five decades ago that the world would be better governed as ten regions due to the perceived human limits to economic and population growth, and backed it up with millions of computer simulations today that go back to the 1970s !

The Club of Rome states the following "Although the effort may initially focus on the implications of growth, particularly of population growth, the totality of the world "problematique" will soon have to be addressed. We believe in fact that the need will quickly become evident for *social innovation* to match technical change, for *radical reform* of institutions and political processes at all levels, including the highest, that of world polity. We are confident that our generation will accept this challenge if we understand the tragic consequences that inaction may bring."

In other words, the CoR has served as the new "prophets" to the United Nations and the world in general, as underlined by Prince Philip, consort of Queen Elizabeth of England in a speech to the CoR : "No generation has ever liked its prophets, least of all those who point out the consequences of bad judgment and lack of foresight. The Club of Rome can take pride in the fact that it has been unpopular for the last twenty years. I hope it will continue many years to come to spell out the unpalatable facts and to unsettle the conscience of *the smug and the apathetic*".

The globalist approach of the Club of Rome is also manifested in its disdain for nationalism and individual sovereignty. Indeed they quote Arnold Toynbee: "The cult of sovereignty has become mankind's major religion. Its God demands human sacrifice". CoR concurs in stating that the erosion of sovereignty may be a positive move towards the new global system for most countries, in which the nation state should have *diminishing significance.*

The spiritual and ethical dimension is no longer an object of scorn or indifference, but is perceived as a necessity that should lead to a **new humanism.**

In their report "Mankind at the Turning Point", the CoR have exposed the running of computer simulations complete with extremely detailed graphs on a variety of human economic and social variables fitted to a world model all the way from the 1970s till now(this process is still ongoing with updated reports today). They claim to predict that there will be a worldwide collapse of human civilization by the mid-21st century or 2050. This they have done by extrapolating those variables forward as quantified by almost 200,000 mathematical equations! To avoid this expected end of the planet under Man, they created a follow-up proposal in a second report.

The world is to be divided into 10 major regions for governance as stated in the "Regionalized and Adaptive Model of the Global World System" report proposed by the CoR in its September 17, 1973 report

These "kingdoms" or regions are proposed as follows:

Group 1: North America

Group 2: Western Europe

Group 3: Japan

Group 4: Rest of the developed market economies including South Africa and Australia

Group 5: Russia and Eastern Europe

Group 6: Latin America

Group 7: North Africa and the Middle East

Group 8: Main Africa

Group 9: South and South east Asia

Group 10: Centrally Planned Asia including China and Mongolia

In order to be able to deal with the complex of factors involved in a way which is sound, credible and systematic, a hierarchical structure has been adopted for the model in which each level in the hierarchy represents the evolution of the world system within a context defined by a given set of laws and principles.

Specifically, the levels involved are:

(1) Geo-physical

(2) Ecological

(3) Technological including man-made energy and mass transfers

(4) Economic

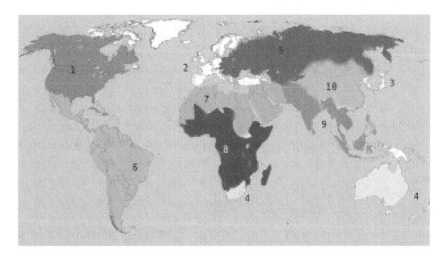

(5) Institutional
(6) Sociopolitical
(7) Value-cultural
(8) Human-biological

The model supposedly deals with a number of critical issues, such as world population growth and effective birth control programs, energy resources utilization and food demand and production and assigns different goals to each of the ten regional groups above.

The authors stated that "the world system is represented in terms of interdependent regional systems, these sub-systems are themselves represented in terms of complete physical, ecological, technological, economic and social descriptions and allowance is made for the capacity of a living system to avert or minimize predicted calamities"

That is, Earth or "Gaia"(named after the Mother Earth goddess) is seen as a living organism that needs *to be fed and nurtured* by these new human and ecological systems.

A large number of different scenarios were fed into the

model which concluded that the "resultant ideal sustainable population is hence more than 500 million but less than one billion." Imagine that! And if you recall that currently the world population is at 7 billion, after some amount of depopulation after World War 3, this agenda might just become popular if only to keep the limit close to the numbers in the report.

The rise of eco-spirituality

In support of the spiritual and ethical dimension of supporting this living Gaia or Earth "organism", they suggest an alliance between all progressive religionists, to lead humanity into a utopia of humanist hope. Today this kind of thinking has resulted in the rapid rise of eco-spirituality (witness the popularity of the book "A New Earth" by Eckhart Tolle and others) and eco-religious movements even extending to elementary school students with programs such as "Care for creation" or "Environmental justice".

After the last war, the 10 overseers of the final world government will also be selected from the corporate and political worlds, possibly from the older Club of Rome, or perhaps more likely today from the newer Club of Madrid, that was created from the CoR and claims to be the single largest group of ex-ruling politicians of the world with "real world" experience. At this point it is too early to tell -We know its coming soon.

Much like with Brussels and the EU, the common citizenry of each region will rarely have their needs met while the elites in the capitals of these regions will enjoy the fruits of the rest. For most of the citizenry, it will be a case of "out of sight, out of mind".

In previous times in the 20th century even more gory accounts of this so-called central management of resources under the Communists have emerged from the annals of the Soviets and the Chinese. In the Soviet Union, it was gleaned from KGB secret files, that the Ukraine went through a devastating famine during the 1930s, resulting in deaths of many Ukrainians and purported cannibalization of the young by their own parents in order to survive. At that time Stalin ruthlessly crushed subsequent attempts at revolution in the Soviet Union and the Ukraine in particular. Stalin would in turn provide inspiration to North Korea's own Stalinist regime in creating harsh punishments for generations of those who fell afoul of the state, right down to the present day.

China's own famine in the 1950s killed 45 million Chinese, not counting the tens of millions who later died under Mao's cultural revolution in the 1960s. Romania's and Nikolai Caucescu's own communist gallery of horrors and dying babies in ill-equipped hospitals is only too well known. Living in central or capital regions away from the penury and misery of the outskirts of each of the world's ten demarcated regions will be recommended during this time.

During the rule of the Antichrist even after the devastation of World War 3, three overseers refuse to implement the progressive agenda in their regions - these are the overseers of Eurasian Russia and the Central Asian Republics, Africa and the Middle East that continue to resist the progressive agenda forced upon them. These three are overthrown overnight by the Antichrist.

The Age of Aquarius

By this time the US, Oceania and Europe have overwhelmingly elected progressive leaders after the last devastating world war. All remaining regions of the world also move under progressive leadership, the democracies being first to move swiftly and lastly the non-democratic countries under coercion from their regional overseer. The progressive spiritual leader based in the world's spiritual capital declares the beginning of the New Age of Aquarius.

This long awaited Age of Aquarius is a "New" age in which

organized religion is considered offensive and rebellion in the cause of "enlightenment" is actively encouraged. Progressive representatives of all the world's religions have their offices in the newly declared spiritual capital. New religious educational programs are announced for the young and these education programs are mandatory. Home schooling is banned entirely and any home schooling parents are thrown into jail and their children taken away from them by social services. Children are taught to resist their conservative parents through reeducation with the new core curriculum. Parents have no say whatsoever in the raising of their children, who are increasingly indoctrinated by a perverse agenda.

Orthodox versions of Abrahamic religions are banned in the public square due to their opposition to abortion, euthanasia, institutionalized immorality and adherence to conservative principles. New progressive versions of the Christian, Islamic and Jewish books are proposed with rewriting of the holy books of these religions to expunge "offensive" verses, punishable by the law.

The progressive agenda of redefining families, marriage and hurting perceived conservatives and their businesses with punitive laws continues unabated till everyone adheres to the "common" world law. Churches split into conservative and progressive factions. Progressives stand for eco-friendly, carbon footprint reducing, gender neutral god, abortion, euthanasia and unrestricted freedom to institutionalize immoral behavior, if only to loosen the bonds of family in the interest of the progressive state. Conservative factions disappear underground overnight along with true versions of the Bible. However the three and a half year countdown also begins for the so-called 2100 year New Age of Aquarius to come to an abrupt end.

""Behold, days are coming," declares the Lord God,

"When I will send a famine on the land,
Not a famine for bread or a thirst for water,
But rather for hearing the words of the Lord."" **Amos 8:11**
(NASB)

CHAPTER 9
Of the Corporate, By the Corporate and For the Corporate

THROUGHOUT HISTORY, HUMANS have attempted to find and create a perfect system of government from the beginnings of the first families on earth. This has the case from the formation of tribes to the inhabitation of new cities with the invention of agriculture through to the modern industrial revolution and even the computer age and the new age of artificial intelligence. In the process we have gone through systems of government from monarchy/aristocracy, theocracy, autocracy, and finally democracy in all their varied forms. These political systems have influenced economic systems in each country into the different forms of feudalism, socialism and capitalism.

Corporatocracy - a new system of worldwide governance emerges

After the end of World War 3, remaining power will be firmly in the hands of those who have money to finance the massive reconstruction efforts of the nations, that is the global corporates. Unlike in previous cases where the form of government eventually determined or undermined the current economic system, the devastating reality in the aftermath of World War 3 will demand an entirely new form of government (corporatocracy). In this system the moneyed corporate leaders will also be the chief officers rebuilding and running the entire world, for the first(and the last) time in human history. These corporates want full global mobility and peace throughout the world, only under their dictates. To this end, the mainstream media will also co-operate to create a new perception of reality, that may be very different to what really is, around the world. In other words it will be corporatocratic fascism at its best.

For those who even in the land of the free and the brave think it impossible, consider this - presently the United States is considered already corporatocratic in its governance, with lobbies of corporations influencing senators and House representatives in Congress to enact laws favorable to industry that in turn provide them with money for reelections. Many senators and House representatives have cornered massive lobby money to the extent that they can be reelected every midterm for life, unlike the US President !

So the corporatocratic concept is nothing new, the only difference being that the corporates will move invisibly from the stage of the United States Congress to that of the World itself as a whole, this time quite visibly. The World will then be run of the Corporate, by the Corporate and for the Corporate. Religion and morals will matter little in this new world. And all this will happen in a surprisingly short period of time of years, courtesy of ongoing advances in artificial intelligence and the prior breakdown of nations in World War 3. The process will be speeded up indeed, if atleast to prevent any World War 4 from happening in the future.

From 2024-25, agendas are in place to guarantee minimum income to unemployed adults of employable age. Abortion, euthanasia and a new freedom of choice called "early checkout" for "bored" or otherwise "useless" people like mentally disabled or handicapped individuals of limited use to the state or the corporate is provided. An age limit of 75 is proposed as detailed in one of the books from an ex-Harvard professor treated as a Bible for the "healthcare" vision of the new corporate age.

The "early checkout" or euthanasia after 75 option is only provided for the common people and not required of the elites who are deemed too important to humanity and not as easily expendable. These common people who choose to check out will be offered to rebuild their lives from scratch in a future humanoid that will use their family and personal history from social media and other websites they used during their lives. This will turn out even at that time to be nothing more than a pipe dream.

The four horsemen of tech

In the mid-2020s, the four horsemen of tech, namely, Google, Facebook, Amazon and (surprise) Amazon Health Services or a massive health-care company run by Amazon will practically provide complete platforms for both corporates and the technological, social, health and shopping needs of individuals in the West. Contrary to expectations, Apple will decline in importance as phone penetration reaches saturation levels and technology moves to the cloud, reducing complexity at the human user end. Every other company will have a connection to these global tech behemoths with services running on their clouds.

Cybernetic implants or tech tattoos(tats) are proposed to be implanted in human beings into the brain's decision making frontal lobe and near the wrist. The tech tat serves both as a self authentication mechanism against "terrorist" forgery and interestingly a way to provide electronic impulses directly to the frontal lobe of the brain to modulate anger or other "negative" emotions in individuals, similar but more powerful than the use of psychoactive drugs or even marijuana and cannabis. However the main reason to provide these tech tats is to keep tabs on everyone and to serve for the loosening of rigid moral braces in individuals making them amenable to state control.

Conservatives refuse to accept these implants and unplug from the system, going underground. Conservatives form underground conclaves where they live on a system of sharing and barter just as in the old days of Christendom when the earliest adherents met in secret to encourage and help each other. Several conservatives establish a cyber currency system for their use to help in operating in a parallel underground economy. However this too is undermined by the new electronic authentication system in place. Cyber currency that once was regulated is now regularly hacked by the massively intelligent QC (quantum computer) system. "Unapproved" transactions are routinely undermined and traced by the government with unsupervised AI.

By this time few use PCs while the vast majority of the world is connected to massive computing and data storage clouds by simpler devices on their person with user interfaces that mostly utilize the power of the cloud for transactions and knowledge mining. Paper money and currency is fully banned worldwide -all money is now transferred digitally. This is all possible entirely now because of the breakdown of governments in World War 3.

All buying and selling of basic services is controlled by a digital conglomerate consisting of Amazon companies. Amazon and its own health services company hold massive data on buying and selling patterns as well as health records of individuals worldwide. Conservatives turn to alternative treatments like homeopathy and natural medicine, making and growing secretly their own herbs, sharing medicines and grown food in a vast underground network that runs on cyber currency and goodwill.

Anyone using the web can no longer anonymously transact. The massively intelligent QC system can decrypt any private conversation by any individual anywhere in the world. Private encryption keys can be instantly broken by this massive computing system and all conversations can be heard live and parsed for anti-government sentiment. The quantum computer with its massive complexity and advanced cooling systems cannot be reproduced except by states or corporates with large funds.

Additionally the quantum communications transmitter by its very nature can sense when its transmissions are being snooped on as the digital bits at the transmitter and receiver are effectively "entangled", making it impossible for man-in-the-middle observers to hack into the system as the QC effectively drops such "observed" transmissions. No one can buy and sell anymore without the computer generated mobile codes authenticated by each user - the key is generated on the tech tat on the wrist or the cybernetic implant on the forehead to identify the user transmitting and receiving. Everything is intruded upon by this AI system to parse user intent and search for sentiment inimical to the agenda of the central world government. It is the job of each of the ten regional overseers to squelch any anti-government sentiment quickly and effectively.

"The Matrix" Redux
With the massively intelligent quantum computer(QC) system, no transactions can be hacked anymore by Anonymous groups or non-state actors. The only hacker is now the QC system. Conservatives stay away from cyber currency, now fully regulated and use barter and collectively live in hiding, similar to the earliest days of the Christians in the catacombs in Europe.

Technological advances that will impact human behavior by the mid 2020s
Several technological advances have been predicted by this time, by an early AI pioneer, Ray Kurzweil that have mostly come true in time with some exceptions. These are elaborated below:
A top of the line personal electronic device a decade in the future will be 1,000 times more powerful than the human brain. Computer implants designed for direct connection to the brain will also be available. They will be capable of augmenting natural senses and of enhancing higher brain functions like memory,

learning speed and overall intelligence.

Computers will be capable of learning and creating new knowledge entirely on their own and with no human help. By scanning the enormous content of the Internet, some computers will know literally every single piece of public information (every scientific discovery, every book and movie, every public statement, etc.) generated by human beings and can even glean what they are possibly up to at any time. This will be encouraged by the Government to weed out "criminal" elements on intentions ahead of concretized action. Think of Google Now reading your next thoughts on search even before you type but vastly more intelligent and preemptive.

Direct brain implants will allow users to enter full-immersion virtual reality--with complete sensory stimulation--without any external equipment. The use of direct brain implants in the brain's frontal lobe(essentially behind the forehead) was seen by the Apostle John 2000 years ago.

"It also forced all people, great and small, rich and poor, free and slave, to receive a mark on their right hands or on their foreheads, so that they could not buy or sell unless they had the mark, which is the name of the beast or the number of its name." **Revelation 13:16-17 (NIV)**

Most communication will occur between humans and machines as opposed to human-to-human. The rise of Artificial Intelligence will create a real "robot rights" movement, and there will be open, public debate over what sorts of civil rights and legal protections machines should have. The existence of humans with heavy levels of cybernetic augmentation and of larger numbers of other people with less extreme cybernetic implants will lead to further arguments over what constitutes a "human being."

Meanwhile as after Roe vs Wade, the number of abortions

worldwide of human foetuses will continue to increase. In order to loosen familial ties and cause differences in the family in support of the corporate state, just as in the communist systems before it, a hedonistic lifestyle will be encouraged, that will include polygamous relationships and relationships with simulated interactive robots, something that even now is starting to happen.

What will not happen in technological advances
Ray Kurzweil who was an early pioneer in optical and speech pattern recognition predicted that human beings would be able to choose new bodies as they got older by means of downloading their memories during their life into social media like Facebook using pictures, thoughts expressed in writings or recordings and videos. These could then be uploaded to new electronic humanoid bodies that would not age or could have parts replaced as required, enabling them theoretically to live forever. This reasoning on the part of Kurzweil was based on his own understanding of Swedenborgian religious principles where the spirit or soul experiences of individuals could transcend the physical and intellectual limitations of their biology.

When you consider that each human being thinks about 75,000 thoughts a day, no machine or earth can capture a single human being in his essence. This dream of Ray Kurzweil is likely just that, an unrealizable pipe dream. We can discount Ray Kurzweil's thoughts on the working of human anatomy as he is not a biologist by training.

On the flip side, Google's Life labs are working to increase human longevity to beyond the current observed maximum at present. The design of the human body today is such that the process of continuous cell division(mitosis) to provide fresh cells can occur only as far a chromosomal tail called telomere does not run out for each cell. After this the cell can no longer divide and dies, failing organs one by one, in what we call a normal human end following a ripe old age. Mathematicians in bioscience who have studied the aging process have come to the remarkable conclusion that any attempt to increase longevity is dealing with a cellular competition where only one side will win, amounting to a catch-22 situation.

Google researchers have pinned hopes on reversing the inevitable decay of biochemistry by repairing DNA or extending the telomeres. Then a number of cells start to populate like there's no tomorrow, reproducing in uncontrolled ways that look too close to cancer. According to the mathematicians, this means we are doomed either way - if we get rid of those poorly functioning, sluggish cells that define old age, then that allows cancer cells to proliferate. So biological researchers ignoring the math may eventually find that human bodies cannot theoretically be extended significantly beyond the maximum at present.

A doctor in Italy has been attempting to do a head transplant from an old person who wants to live longer into a new body. Suffice it to say, that a decade later he is still trying, giving the lie to Kurzweil's own vision of the future human body. None of these expected advances will come to fruition now or in the future.

CHAPTER 10
Antichrist Emerges - A New Adam

THE FIGURE OF THE FINAL ANTICHRIST has always baffled and intrigued Christians from the time of John's revelations. The revelations of St John while impressively futuristic in their vision were not understood by Christians for almost 1900 years, till the dawn of the internet age. As electronics and wireless communications become more miniaturized, the picture has finally emerged on how the Antichrist will run his all-pervasive system of buying and selling and exert complete control over the basic needs of all human beings on earth, save those who do not enter his system.

The Antichrist has been deemed at any point of time to be anyone from Kissinger to Saddam Hussein to Khomeini and even a fictional Romanian from the EU named Nikolai or an Assyrian or future caliph from the Islamic state. However it is clear from the book of Revelation that the Antichrist is someone who can be identified by his number, the very foreboding "666", a number skipped in fear on everything from hotel room numbers to license number plates today. While undecipherable to Christians till the end of the 20th century, today this number from the apostle John is already visible, in full view of the unsuspecting Christian .

And what is this now ubiquitous "666", you may ask ? For this we start from the Creation of Man as described in the book of Genesis.

"Then God said, "Let us make mankind in our image, in our likeness, so that they may rule over the fish in the sea and the birds in the sky, over the livestock and all the wild animals, and over all the creatures that move along the ground. So God created mankind in his own image, in the image of God he created them; male and female he created them." **Genesis 1:26-27** *(NIV)*

The creation of Man occurs on the sixth day. The number 6 signifies Imperfect Man just as 7 signifies the perfection of God, starting with God's admonition that the seventh day be kept holy and dedicated to Him alone.

Remember that Satan, the adversary of Man and God is a counterfeiter. He copies everything that God does, including the very act of Creation in order to populate his kingdom with his acolytes. This is clear throughout the Bible where in the book of Genesis God marks Cain with a special mark to other men to avoid him as a murderer. In the Book of Revelation, Satan copies this gesture to mark those who will belong to his kingdom.

"It also forced all people, great and small, rich and poor, free and slave, to receive a mark on their right hands or on their foreheads, so that they could not buy or sell unless they had the mark, which is the name of the beast or the number of its name." **Revelation 13:16-17** *(NIV)*

The whole industrial and technological revolution in the last 150 years comes to a head towards this one goal. And to this end some men have expected that a historical singularity - (perfected) AI or artificial intelligence to emerge that will eventually destroy humanity. Yes, some of the top technological and scientific leaders and geniuses of our time including Elon Musk and Stephen Hawking actually believe this.

The trinity from Hell

Here is the act of pseudo-creation all over again - the number 6, referring to Man repeated thrice for emphasis. The number refers to a new creation in the image of Satan himself, of Man, by Man and for Man (666) to subjugate and enslave in his new kingdom. Satan will become the new "creator"or "Father" and Antichrist will then become the New "Adam" or "Son". The false prophet who supports the Beast or Antichrist signifies the "spiritual" or third aspect of this unholy trinity. Once again the dragon or Satan sets up a counterfeit to the Holy trinity of God the Father, the Son and the Holy Spirit.

Note the co-opting of the Christian Trinity is not a new thing. Even in modern history, a counterfeit trinity had been institutionalized as the state sanctioned religion of "Juche" by the founder of North Korea Kim Il-Sung. This unholy trinity had him as the "eternal Father", the "Son" represented by his own son Kim Jong-Il and the binding "spirit" being the wife of Kim il-Sung, that is, the mother of Jong-Il. Kim Il Sung actually grew up in a Christian home with a pastor for a grandfather and a church elder for a father ! The state religion of Juche now teaches North Koreans that after death they will be reunited with Kim il-Sung forever.

And so the leaders of men continue to do the same as they have done in previous ages.

"What has been will be again, what has been done will be done again; there is nothing new under the sun."
Ecclesiastes 1:9 *(NIV)*

We will now derive the name that the Antichrist's number refers to. Be assured, the name will be nothing new to you who have come of age in the last two decades and a half. It will be clear in a moment.

There will be no number tricks or games to force the number from a name, no use of Hebrew gematria or numerology or any such superstitious games of numbers or years. The Bible specifically frowns on these practices so why should we engage in them ? Do you think that the apostle John really hoped Christians would dabble in numerology to decipher his revelations ? Of course not!

In previous times, people considered Kissinger to be 666. Names like Bill Clinton or even Ronald Reagan were wrestled with numerologically to form 666, depending on where your political emotions lay. Suffice it to say, that you could take the name Peter Jensen and squeeze and cajole it to form a 666 in some numerical system worldwide. You could even use your own full name and get it to form 666 in some language or numerical system. Does this mean that you or I are the Antichrist - God forbid! But you get the point. The Bible is sweet and simple. It is we who play these complicated games with simple verses. We will return to the Book of Revelation. We will quote from the original King James version because the original verse is especially important here and can be interpreted differently from the modern yet different rendition of the same.

"Here is wisdom. Let him that hath understanding **count** *the number of the beast: for it is the number of a man; and his number is Six hundred threescore and six."* **Revelation 13:18** *(KJV)*

The modern versions have the number of the beast as "calculated"(when in doubt always go back to the original King James). This is however unlikely to be what the apostle John meant when he put down his vision. Just think of the likelihood of the apostle juxtapositioning numbers from the letters of a name and adding it all up to get 666 while receiving the vision. And it is also the reason why previous generations have calculated and called out the name of the beast in different ways only to be eventually frustrated as their supposed "beast" passed on with no consequences to the rest of humanity.

We are not asked to numerologically wrestle with or score the number of the Beast but to COUNT it - the number is 6 repeated thrice - signifying clearly yet another counterfeit creation on the lines of the human species by God on the sixth day. Only this time in a "New" age in a new book of Genesis that will begin in Satan's own "bible" where he hopes man will begin again, firmly in his kingdom from this act of pseudo-creation. This Luciferian Age is called the Age of Aquarius, as some religious progressives are eagerly awaiting at this time, to last 2100 years. The Bible also predicts that this New worldwide Age of Aquarius will last for the grand total of exactly - three and a half years! So believers left on earth don't have to wait out the coming persecution too long!

Once that begins, Satan will ape God and create his own Satanic bible for our consumption. Rather than start a whole new bible that no one will believe, he'll simply take ours and substitute himself in them, removing all the grossly "offensive" verses, that pertaining to immorality and the actions that lead to our own self-destruction and everything that "offends" the sinner. Just as once God created Man and gave him laws through which to govern himself.

The meaning of the Antichrist

The apostle John being Jewish dictated his revelations in Hebrew and it is there where we will start to decipher this code. No letter encryption, numerology or numeric circuses with names are involved. Let's start with the Hebrew alphabet. The Hebrew alphabet has 22 letters, of which five have different forms when used at the end of a word. They are given below:

Hebrew is written from right to left, like the other semitic language, Arabic. The 6th alphabet of Hebrew is "Wav", after Aleph, Bet, Geem, Dal and He

Now transposing the alphabet according to the number in the Bible

"666" becomes

"**Wav**" "**Wav**" "**Wav**"

Or **WWW** -> The World Wide Web. "WavWavWav" is also interestingly geek speak for the worldwide web. This was likely what the apostle heard and coded into simple numbers, yet becoming something that would be understandable only in the present day.

As you have seen, I have not brought your attention to vague scribbles on cloth, flags, pieces of breakfast pastry or my kitchen wall to derive some scrawl that resembles '666'. We have decoded it without employing any visual gimmick. For our current and final age before the end of time, it is however clear, isn't it? If it is not, it will be clearer as you continue reading. We know that it is the number of a man. So how is this man connected to WWW ? The Bible with all the wisdom, power and glory contained within is very simple for man to understand. Some of the most beloved and simplest verses in the Bible are the same ones that are the most moving and powerful in their impact like *John 3:16*.

That's just the way God works. It is us human beings who complicate things. It is also the reason why *Revelation 13:18* immediately follows *Revelation 13:17*. They are linked together. If you are surprised why Christians in prior generations could not comprehend it - recall from the foreword earlier in this book that it was meant to be realized only by Christians of the present Internet age who would see it come to fruition in their time. Not even those of the digital and electronic age that started decades earlier in the early and mid 1900s.

The angel who explained the prophet Daniel's visions to him tells us why. Remember that even Daniel who saw the vision did not understand it. It was beyond the technology of his time.

*"And he said, "Go your way, Daniel, for these words are concealed and sealed up **until the end time." Daniel 12:9** (NASB)*

That time is this decade coincidentally before we hit the 2000th anniversary of the crucifixion of our Lord, at the same time that humanity is hitting its technological singularity, an event that is projected to eventually wipe it out on earth. If the Lord does not come quickly, we humans will destroy ourselves before He comes.

We are soon entering the final decade of the Lord's return. So aptly, the Antichrist's meaning is finally revealed. All previous false interpretations of Antichrist have come and gone without us ever seeing them come to fruition.

WWW or the Internet as it is called today has not really been around that long. From its first beginnings in the mid-1990s, it has already revolutionized every aspect of current human existence, becoming common-place in our daily life. It is now seen everywhere, a needed tool without which few can operate. In other words, the internet today is as compulsory as food, water and shelter.

WWW has come a long way from its beginnings as a set of interconnected computers. From there it has evolved into "walled gardens" such as Facebook and Google that billions use in their everyday life, addicted to the flicker of their smartphones and the likes and re-tweets they receive and the reviews their businesses get daily on Facebook and everywhere else. Every other day a new thorny human problem is tackled and interfaced onto a new website on the internet, making it easy and efficient to do everything from the mobile web, or one's own smartphone. The world wide web is now a valuable second skin around our own human skin, one that is impossible to shed and as important as our basic needs.

WWW is slowly evolving into something bigger even as we speak. A certain gaggle of clouds much like the ones you see in the sky today talk and interact with each other. These clouds will interconnect to form one big cloud so that we have one cloud under which everyone will operate daily to buy, sell, check on his health and earn his daily living. And much like the EU was for Europe, this worldwide cloud will have a head - the Antichrist who will create a virtual reality cloud in which we consume the "right" news and work and have our current location known to the cloud. Today's millennials who live in walled off electronic gardens in their parents' houses with their high student debts won't mind this intrusion on their privacy one wee bit. Its a small price to pay for being always connected to new experiences.

So here's what I was talking about in a nutshell, **WWW** is getting into more and more devices and machines - your washing machine, fridge, dishwasher, your key fob and anything else you can think of. Its called the *Internet of Things*(IOT). These things are already all talking to each other or will do so soon. If it can get into every device you have in your house or elsewhere, where do you think it will end up next when these devices are exhausted ? Your guess is correct - in the human **body**, the last frontier for **WWW**. Specifically as the Apostle saw himself - in the forehead or in the hand you move everyday to get things done. Its coming!

Transhumanism, Nimrod revisited and the rise of *Homo Deus*

The only true artificial intelligence at the time will be humans using cybernetic implants, in other words, augmented intelligence or IA (Intelligence Amplification). This is the lie of transhumanism, of a new evolution beyond the flesh.

Transhumanism is the belief that the human race can evolve beyond current physical and mental limitations, by means of science and technology. If you suspect this will never become reality in our generation - you may find that the advanced versions of it may happen sooner than you think, in the next 5-10 years.

Yuval Harari, a well known secular Israeli researcher calls this the human "evolution" from Homo Sapiens ("intelligent human") to *Homo Deus*("human god")

Currently at least two companies, Neuralink from Elon Musk and Kernel from Bryan Johnson are attempting to create a neural "lace", to transmit information via electronic impulses or by light impulses between the neural lace connected to WWW and the human brain on which it will implant. Initial attempts will be to experiment with volunteer patients with end-stage Alzheimer's disease or other neuro-degenerative conditions before working on cognitive enhancements for the average user. This is partly because it is incredibly dangerous and invasive to operate on the human brain, and only those who have exhausted every other medical option choose to undergo such surgery as a last resort.

The initial reasons for starting Neuralink was to stay ahead of the potentially perfect humanoid that other companies were building by ensuring that humans always remained one step ahead of the projected technological "singularity". Obviously Elon Musk is very apprehensive of future humanoids taking over and killing us all. For us today it is easier to envision the possibility of a human with an intelligent implant than an inorganic robot that can outmaneuver our own brains in every sense, that might not materialize at all in our generation.

However, a few tens of thousands of people worldwide already have very basic stimulating electrodes already placed inside their skulls, so the idea is not recent. These simpler electrodes are already used to treat brain disorders like Parkinson's disease. Musk wants to build on that, for very sick patients and later for healthy persons to implant tiny electrodes in the brain "that may one day upload and download thoughts to and from a computer"(in his own words), or by extension WWW or interconnected computers.

By his own admission, Mr. Musk says *"for a meaningful partial-brain interface, I think we're roughly four or five years away."* And the Defense Advanced Research Projects Agency(DARPA) itself is investing $60 million over four years to develop implantable neural interface technology, presumably for the American soldier of the future. We already have bone conducting headsets to "hear" through the skull without hearing and soon will be able to "speak" without actually speaking.

Yet the apostle John saw this in its entirety 2000 years ago, even telling us that some would actually choose such a means of cognitive enhancement in the kingdom of the Antichrist!

The man of iniquity, the ultimate liberal progressive, the Antichrist himself is expected to be an individual with the WWW connected neural implant or The World Wide Cloud master control built into him, the cybernetic "football" so as to speak. With his own adoption of this implant in his forehead, he will urge or force others to join his kingdom by accepting their own implant, either on the forehead or the wrist. He will be the leader of the ten overseers of the world's politically, culturally and economically demarcated regions and these ten overseers will report to him.

Much like the despots of old, the Antichrist will see the need to create a sustainable spiritual blueprint to tie others to his kingdom and will be helped in this by the false prophet, the progressive church leader chosen by progressive religious everywhere. Abortion and euthanasia will then become officially "sacred" in the service of Mother Earth and a reduced human carbon footprint (recently a very progressive House leader in the US has reiterated the "sacred" nature of abortion). Marriages will be perverted while polygamy and polyandrous marriages will be encouraged. It will be like the days of Noah. People will seek evil and take pleasure in the work of other evil-doers.

"For this reason God sends them a powerful delusion so that they will believe the lie and so that all will be condemned who have not believed the truth but have delighted in wickedness." **2 Thessalonians 2:11-12** *(NIV)*

Time is a scroll indeed. We have come back full circle to the times of Noah, only with advanced technology. There is nothing new under the sun.

CHAPTER 11
Mystery Babylon

AT DIFFERENT TIMES IN CHRISTIAN ESCHATOLOGY, the
identity of Mystery Babylon that the apostle John refers to in the
Book of Revelation has been widely implied to be any one of three
or four cities in the world today. Some have referred to a city in
Babylon or present day Iraq, others to to Rome, yet others to
Jerusalem or even Brussels, the current headquarters of the
European Union. More recently in the most odd fashion possible,
Mecca, the holy city of Islam in Saudi Arabia has been named
Mystery Babylon. The understanding of Mystery Babylon has
never been so diversified and no other scripture in Revelation as
much scrutinized. Clues to the characteristics of this city are
provided by the apostle John,

*"One of the seven angels who had the seven bowls came
and said to me, "Come, I will show you the punishment of the
great prostitute, who sits by many waters. With her the kings of
the earth committed adultery, and the inhabitants of the earth
were intoxicated with the wine of her adulteries."*

*Then the angel carried me away in the Spirit into a
wilderness. There I saw a woman sitting on a scarlet beast that
was covered with blasphemous names and had seven heads and
ten horns. **The woman was dressed in purple and scarlet,
and was glittering with gold**, precious stones and pearls. She
held a golden cup in her hand, filled with abominable things and*

the filth of her adulteries. The name written on her forehead was a mystery:

> *Babylon the great*
> *the mother of prostitutes*
> *and of the abominations of the earth." **Revelation 17:1-5** (NIV)*

As early as the European Reformation, Rome has been considered as Mystery Babylon for obvious reasons, as the seat of the Catholic church and apostasy from God. For one, Rome is the original city of seven hills. And it is a city of some great influence at least with Western nations and Catholics that make up a little less than a fifth of the world's population. The Catholic population today is even less than that of Islam, though its power today even with European nations is not as much as it was in the past when it crowned the kings of Europe. As with the European Union, the temporal power of the Catholic church is also declining steadily ever since the European Reformation as individual European countries broke away from the Vatican. Additionally the problem with the reasoning of Rome as Mystery Babylon is clear in the original reading of the verses in the book of Revelation.

*"Then the angel said to me: "Why are you astonished? I will explain to you the mystery of the woman and of the beast she rides, which has the seven heads and ten horns." **Revelation 17:7** (NIV)*

*"Then the angel said to me, "The waters you saw, where the prostitute sits, are peoples, multitudes, nations and languages." **Revelation 17:15** (NIV)*

*"The woman you saw is the great city that rules over the kings of the earth." **Revelation 17:18** (NIV)*

Secular Rome, the capital of Italy sits on seven hills but it is not Mystery Babylon even from a cursory reading of the Revelation 17:9 verse. It is not Mystery Babylon that is described with seven heads or hills *but the Beast* who hates her.

"This calls for a mind with wisdom. The seven heads are seven hills on which the woman sits." **Revelation 17:9** *(NIV)*

Mystery Babylon is described in alliance with the headquarters of the beast that has seven heads (seven hills). This implies that the seat from where the progressive anti-God humanist Beast runs the world is the conveniently central international city of Rome. So it is the defacto international capital chosen by the future Beast and not of the European Union(even now Brussels) which is in tatters by this time. We will revisit this again in the last chapter of this book.

Babylon or Iraq can also not be Mystery Babylon as it refers to a country not a city. Modern Iraq factionalized into Sunni, Shia and other groups is a country of little influence in the world today.

Brussels, the capital of Belgium though the head of the European Union is influential mostly in Europe and not outside the continent. It is also not exactly a center for spirituality as the European union representatives mostly adhere to a doctrine of strict secularity and non-promotion of any religion, including the Christian religion that Europeans confessed widely at times in the past.

Mecca in Saudi Arabia is not exactly a city of worldwide influence. Its influence is mostly restricted to the 57 nations of the Islamic world and to Muslims who make up about one fifth of the worlds' population. The other 80% of the world's population has nothing to do with Mecca or Islam. Which brings us to our final choice for Mystery Babylon, one that has been widely accepted by most of the current Christian scholars today - Jerusalem.

Why Jerusalem is and always will be Mystery Babylon
Jerusalem the holy city from times immemorial has been sacred
to Jews, Christians and Muslims. Numerous wars have been
fought over it, Christ has wept over its prior apostasies and
spiritual prostitution. It is holy to over half of the world's current
population - a tag unique only to it. And in today's world it is
described as a cup that makes the nations dizzy with desire - not
only those surrounding it but located also far away from it, to
those in the Middle East and South and South east Asia, to us in
the United States and those in Russia and in the far corners of
Australia and South America. The prophet Zechariah describes
the dizzying effect that Jerusalem has on the surrounding nations.

*"I am going to make Jerusalem a cup that sends all the
surrounding peoples reeling. Judah will be besieged as well as
Jerusalem. On that day, when all the nations of the earth are
gathered against her, I will make Jerusalem an immovable rock
for all the nations. All who try to move it will injure themselves."*
Zechariah 12:2 *(NIV)*

If ever there was a single city that had a place in mens'
hearts, it is Jerusalem. Almost all the peoples of the world have
their temples and their hearts in it - from the Lutheran,
Evangelical, Orthodox, Pentecostal and various other
denominations of Christianity to the Sunni and Shia Muslims and
of course the Jews themselves.

There is yet another clue as to Jerusalem being Mystery
Babylon. There is a second verse that refers to this "great city" in
the book of Revelation. In the following verse, the "great city" is
also not directly named but clearly understood to be Jerusalem.
Continuing from Revelation 11,

*"Their bodies will lie in the public square of the great city--which is figuratively called Sodom and Egypt--where also their Lord was crucified." **Revelation 11:8-9** (NIV)*

Since the Lord went to Jerusalem to be crucified as the final sin offering without blemish, we know that it is Jerusalem the great city that is referred to as Mystery Babylon.

And again at other places, Jerusalem is identified as the prostitute when the Jewish Temple is described standing there:

*"He said: "Son of man, this is the place of my throne and the place for the soles of my feet. This is where I will live among the Israelites forever. The people of Israel will never again defile my holy name--neither they nor their kings--by their prostitution and the funeral offerings for their kings at their death. When they placed their threshold next to my threshold and their doorposts beside my doorposts, with only a wall between me and them, they defiled my holy name by their detestable practices. So I destroyed them in my anger. Now let them put away from me their prostitution and the funeral offerings for their kings, and I will live among them forever." **Ezekiel 43:7-9** (NIV)*

And if you still doubt it is Jerusalem, here's what I call the clincher. In both Revelation 17:3 and Jeremiah 4:30, there is a reference to the same prostitute with many lovers, **"dressed in scarlet and glittering with gold, precious stones and pearls"**. And just as in the book of Revelation, where the Beast despises Jerusalem and wants to destroy her with fire, the prophet Jeremiah sees the progressive government in Jerusalem after World War 3 continuing to court the godless Beast who despises her and wants to kill her! John and Jeremiah are clearly both referring to Jerusalem with their *perfectly matching* descriptions of the great city.

"What are you doing, you devastated one?
   Why dress yourself in scarlet
   and put on jewels of gold?
Why highlight your eyes with makeup?
   You adorn yourself in vain.
Your lovers despise you;
   they want to kill you." Jeremiah 4:30 (NIV)

Can you understand how God feels about His bride courting her murderous lovers in spite of His own great love for her? You even see how He lets a human being feel this pain He felt, through the prophet Hosea and how this wonderful prophet of God is asked to marry a prostitute called Gomer and yet love her in spite of her harlotry. We can only imagine what pain our ever faithful God feels through the ages on account of Jerusalem.

Again there are other places in the book of Revelation as well as in the Bible where it is clearly stated that Jerusalem will be partially desolated and partially destroyed by its enemies ("they will burn her with fire"). Note, it is possible that during this partial desolation, the current structures on the Temple mount could be destroyed, causing a rebuilding this time in peace of both the third Jewish temple and the mosque on the mount. It is also possible that the new Israeli government with the Middle Eastern regional overseer will bring this about and Antichrist who makes peace between the Jew and the Arab will eventually enthrone himself in the Jewish temple.

"Then the angel said to me, "The waters you saw, where the prostitute sits, are peoples, multitudes, nations and languages. The beast and the ten horns you saw will hate the prostitute. They will bring her to ruin and leave her naked; they will eat her

flesh and burn her with fire."" **Revelation 17:15-16** *(NIV)*

In the end-times the city of Jerusalem is ransacked in the final war on the remnant of the Jews by the forces of the Antichrist, with soldiers drawn from the regions of the closest of the ten overseers, making it a clearly "*global*" army.

"I will gather all the nations to Jerusalem to fight against it; the city will be captured, the houses ransacked, and the women raped. Half of the city will go into exile, but the rest of the people will not be taken from the city."
Zechariah 14:2 *(NIV)*

How is this attempted destruction of Jerusalem still happening after World War 3 has just ended a few years ago? Will the Jews ever receive any respite from a long lineup of enemies through the ages? Israel's enemy Gog has already been destroyed along with all his allies by coalition forces including the United States, its reluctant allies in Europe and Israel. How this new and final attempt to wipe out the Jews globally will come about will become clearer in the next few chapters.

CHAPTER 12
Final destruction of the Jews plotted in peacetime

A FEW MONTHS BEFORE HE DIED in 2006 at the age of 108, one of Israel's most prominent rabbis, Yitzhak Kaduri surprised his followers when he told them that he met the Messiah. Kaduri gave a message in his synagogue on Yom Kippur, the Day of Atonement, teaching how to recognize the Messiah.

He wrote the name of the Messiah on a small note which he requested would remain sealed until after his death. When the note was unsealed, it revealed what many have known for centuries: Yehoshua, or Yeshua (Jesus), is the Messiah.

Rabbi Yitzhak Kaduri was known for his photographic memory and his memorization of the Bible, the Talmud and other Jewish writings. He knew the Jewish sages of the last century and the rabbis who lived in the Holy Land and kept the faith alive before the State of Israel was even born.

The Rabbi described the Messiah using six words, hinting that the initial letters form the name of the Messiah. The secret note said:

"Concerning the letter abbreviation of the Messiah's name, He will lift the people and prove that his word and law are valid.
This I have signed in the month of mercy,
Yitzhak Kaduri"

The Hebrew sentence (translated above in bold) with the hidden name of the Messiah reads:

Yarim **H**a'Am **V**eyokhiakh **S**hedvaro **V**etorato **O**mdim

spelling *Yehoshua* or *Yeshua, the Hebrew for Jesus*)

Jewish admirers of the late Rabbi responded to this with mixed feelings. The event was quickly swept under the carpet and his website scrubbed of any references to the secret note lest the Jews in Israel got any more ideas.

Growing realization among the Jews

There is however a growing realization among at least some Jews that the Messiah has already come - he who the Jews were waiting for, as prophesied by the Jewish prophets 2000 years ago with the exact time line for his first coming indicated by the prophet Daniel's 70 weeks prophecy.

Throughout the centuries Jews attempting to place notable rabbis in the role of Messiah have failed, from Simon bar Kokhba who led a short-lived Jewish state against the Romans in the 2nd century to a Yemenite messiah who actually pleaded to be beheaded by the Muslim authorities on the 12th century so he could come back to life. The last being Menachem Mendel Schneerson in the 20th century, the only Messiah who did not know he was a Messiah and denied it when his followers told him so, till the day he died !

Attempted genocides against the Jews in ancient and modern history

The Jews have been fighting enemies bent on their destruction from the beginnings of their father Jacob (later named Israel or "he who wrestles with God"). For one thing Satan wanted to use Esau to kill his brother Jacob. There was another attempted genocide of the Jews throughout the Persian empire by the right-hand man Haman of Emperor Ahasuerus of Persia. It was his queen Esther, a Jewess and her uncle who had forestalled this genocide at the very last moment. This was after Ahasuerus's decree had already gone out unwittingly to eliminate the Jews throughout his empire. At that time there were not yet many Jews in Europe.

Not to be outdone by the Persians, after this came the Roman destruction of the Jewish temple in 70 AD, exactly 40 years after the crucifixion of Christ, with the killings of over 1 million Jews and the forced diaspora of the remnant of the Jews as slaves into Europe. This was again an attempt to erase the history and culture of the Jews.

Later in the 20th century, the vastly efficient, organized and methodical German Nazis under Hitler killed six million Jews preceding and during World War II in the Holocaust, in the concentration camps and the gas ovens. Now it appears with the furious Iranian government of today under the current Shiite mullahs still want to liquidate every last one of them.

Sadly in the past even zealous Christians have carried out pogroms against the Jews, by taking too literally the charge against them of deicide, from massacres of Jews all across the Byzantine empire to the Catholic Inquisitions in Spain to Martin Luther's eight-point plan to get rid of the Jews by forced religious conversion or expulsion. It is clear however that it is rather all of us who have crucified Christ on account of our sins. And Christ has paid the price already for all of us.

Yet even today, the Israelis can handle all their enemies including the Iranians on their own with a little help from the United States. And yet there is that other insurmountable enemy after that to come - literally all the nations on earth ! Mathew 23:29 merely states that the only one who can save them from this seemingly endless cycle of enemies is Jesus Himself but only if they call out to Him. This currently the Orthodox Jew will never do, of course.

In 1930s Germany, Hitler and the Nazi party proposed a final solution for the Jews - his solution was the extermination of Jews not only in Germany, but also in Europe and elsewhere. He wanted countries everywhere to give up their Jews for elimination through his concentration camps and gas ovens. But was Hitler doing it out of his Christian zeal or was there something else ?

The early youth of Hitler and his initiation into the occult gives a clue to what this other influence was. The monk turned occultist Lenz mentored Hitler and brought him in contact with the teachings of the Theosophist Madame Blavatsky. This is no attempt whatsoever to whitewash the works of a few so-called Christian leaders who stood with Hitler during this subjugation and extermination campaign against the Jews. These so called "Christian" leaders - a few German Lutherans, Catholics and others were impressed by Hitler's new Aryan religion in which he would become its future high priest and leader.

Indeed during Hitler's reign as the chancellor, many churches had their bibles and crosses forcibly removed and replaced with Hitler's book, the "Mein Kampf" and a sword instead of the cross. Here was a new religion - albeit an ancient ruse of the devil built on godless Nietzschean philosophy and remodeled after Helena Blavatsy's occult heresies. For in the writings of Madame Blavatsky, the Jews were an inferior root race that needed to be weeded out once and for all to make way for the new human race. It was the new super race that humanity would evolve into, once the Jews were gone and the Christian religion was replaced by that based on the old rites.

Nietzsche's nihilistic philosophy of the survival of the fittest and the weeding out of the genetic "undesirables" would guide the evolution of the new race. Surely there was nothing remotely Christian or even Abrahamic in that wish! Abraham cared for the poor and the disadvantaged and welcomed strangers into his home. All three major Abrahamic religions - Christianity, Judaism and Islam have always tried to follow Abraham in this spirit, even if not always charitably toward each other, atleast to those of their own kind.

No respite for the Jews

Coming back again to the late 2020s, this genocidal instinct against the Jews will come to the fore once again for the last time. This will not let up even after the devastating world war ends amidst a previous attempted destruction of Israel by Iran and its allies. A remnant of Jewish progressive leaders will take over the interim Israeli government after World War 3.

Who are some of these progressive Jewish leaders ? It would be surprising to know that some Jews today are so progressive that the anti-Zionist party called Neturei Karta made up of these actively campaign against the "Zionist" state and meet with the enemies of the Israel in Iran on a regular basis. You can imagine what would happen if they took over ! There is no dearth of less radical progressive parties in Israel even today, who believe peace is possible with all Arab nations without sacrificing Israel.

Israel's ultra progressive leadership, the fall of the Wall and Psalm 83

When Israel is also taken over by a radically progressive government that seeks peace with the remnant of the Sunni Arabs under the new overseer of the Middle Eastern region after WW3, it has a progressive female leader in the endtimes(as prophesied in *Isaiah 4*). The Antichrist will **then** succeed in making peace between the Arab and the Jew.

To this end, He will request his Middle East overseer to bring down the so-called "apartheid" wall between Israel and the Arab territories among popular requests from the majority and progressive leadership on the Israeli side. However the Orthodox Jews will not relent for new progressive laws to be imposed on them and the relaxation of borders with the Arabs. Orthodox Jews resist any compromise on Jewish security but are pushed aside by the progressives who pledge their support to the Middle East region's new overseer. Walls are broken down between Israel and Syria and between Jewish and Arab enclaves in Israel and the Palestinian territories.

Seeing their chance the Sunni Arabs in the regions surrounding Israel in Jordan, Lebanon and others will attack to destroy the Jews and take over their lands once and for all. Iran and Turkey(both non-Arab countries) having been destroyed and devastated earlier are nowhere in the picture this time. The Psalmist Asaph gives us the names of the Middle Eastern Arab nations aligned against God and His hidden ones(as rendered in the original KJV):

> *"With cunning they conspire against your people;*
> *they plot against those you cherish.*
> *"Come," they say, "let us destroy them as a nation,*
> **so that Israel's name is remembered no more."**
> *With one mind they plot together;*
> *they form an alliance against you--*
> *the tents of Edom and the Ishmaelites,*
> *of Moab and the Hagrites,*
> *Byblos, Ammon and Amalek,*
> *Philistia, with the people of Tyre.*
> *Even Assyria has joined them*
> *to reinforce Lot's descendants." **Psalm 83:3-8** (NIV)*

Like the Psalmist Asaph, Ezekiel also talks of this uprising of the Sunni Arabs against the Jews in Israel at the endtimes, naming Edom(Jordan), Teman to Dedan (Arabia), allies of the United States in World War 3. The Ishmaelites in Psalm 83 refer to the Arab tribes that came forth from Ishmael, the son of the slave of Abraham, also spread among ancient Arabia.

Tyre(a city in Lebanon) refers to the Lebanese. Byblos like Tyre sits north of Beirut in Lebanon. Hagrites are possibly Egyptians as they are connected to Hagar, the Egyptian mother of Ishmael. Amalek and Gebal are the perpetual enemies of Israel among the regions of its immediate Arab neighbors. And Philistia denotes the Philistines with a substantial presence east of Gaza in Palestinian territory today.

At this time, the Middle East has its own overseer and so does the United States.

"This is what the Sovereign Lord says: 'Because Edom took revenge on Judah and became very guilty by doing so, therefore this is what the Sovereign Lord says: I will stretch out my hand against Edom and kill both man and beast. I will lay it waste, and from Teman to Dedan they will fall by the sword. I will take vengeance on Edom by the hand of my people Israel, and they will deal with Edom in accordance with my anger and my wrath; they will know my vengeance, declares the Sovereign Lord.'" **Ezekiel 25:12-14** *(NIV)*

And again, very clearly, this is happening at a time when Israel is already past a calamitous war. These Sunni Arab nations have escaped major devastation by standing clear of the war against Israel, allied with the United States against Iran, but refusing to defend Israel against Iran and Turkey as a matter of perpetual enmity with the Jews. These nations now see a chance to overwhelm the remnant of the Jews in Israel when "they are laid desolate" in the last war and the walls have been brought down between Israel and the Arabs to be administered under a single Middle Eastern overseer.

"The word of the Lord came to me: "Son of man, set your

face against Mount Seir; prophesy against it and say: 'This is what the Sovereign Lord says: I am against you, Mount Seir, and I will stretch out my hand against you and make you a desolate waste. I will turn your towns into ruins and you will be desolate. Then you will know that I am the Lord.

"'Because you harbored an ancient hostility and delivered the Israelites over to the sword at the time of their calamity, the time their punishment reached its climax, therefore as surely as I live, declares the Sovereign Lord, I will give you over to bloodshed and it will pursue you. Since you did not hate bloodshed, bloodshed will pursue you. I will make Mount Seir a desolate waste and cut off from it all who come and go.'"
Ezekiel 35:1-7 (NIV)

Again Ezekiel mentions that these nations that cherished perpetual enmity against Israel rejoice over the "inheritance" of partially desolated tiny Israel, presumably at this time by being the majority population in the Middle East, using qualified majority voting rules used previously in other governing entities, like the European Union.

"'Because you have said, "These two nations and countries will be ours and we will take possession of them," even though I the Lord was there, therefore as surely as I live, declares the Sovereign Lord, I will treat you in accordance with the anger and jealousy you showed in your hatred of them and I will make myself known among them when I judge you. Then you will know that I the Lord have heard all the contemptible things you have said against the mountains of Israel. You said, "They have been laid waste and have been given over to us to devour." You boasted against me and spoke against me without restraint, and I heard it. This is what the Sovereign Lord says: While the whole earth rejoices, I will make you desolate. Because you rejoiced

*when the inheritance of Israel became desolate, that is how I will treat you. You will be desolate, Mount Seir, you and all of Edom. Then they will know that I am the Lord."' **Ezekiel 35:10-15 (NIV)***

However their rejoicing is short-lived as the Lord deals with them directly for their unending enmity against the Jews.

The Psalmist Asaph gives us their final fate in the same Psalm 83, as they conspire against God and His hidden Ones:

"Do to them as you did to Midian,
 as you did to Sisera and Jabin at the river Kishon,
 who perished at Endor
 and became like dung on the ground." Psalm 83:9-10(NIV)

Final treachery and the end of the Jews planned

The Palestinians encouraged by their fellow Sunni Arab brethren in the Arabian states, Jordan, Lebanon and Assyria (today in Iraq) see this as a chance to overwhelm Israel either by numbers or by striking when they have the chance with Israel's guard down. The Orthodox Jews who stick to their weapons are threatened by the Antichrist for resisting peace and he commands his Middle Eastern overseer to correct the situation. Due to the heavy weaponry possessed by the Orthodox Jews, only a limited Arab response to take out the Jewish defences is possible.

The new overseer of the Middle East will request help from the other nearby overseers in Europe, Africa and Russia to put down the Jewish rebellion - but the aim of the Antichrist is to secretly to wipe out the remnant of the Jews once and for all before the return of Jesus. Satan once again aims cunningly to hold God to His Word in the Bible.

*"For I tell you, you will not see me again **UNTIL** you say, 'Blessed is he who comes in the name of the Lord.'" **Matthew 23:39** (NIV)*

For this saying of Christ specifically to the Jews has been on Satan's mind from the very beginning, to forestall the Son of God from returning to earth and overthrowing his own kingdom using the verses of the Bible as a guarantor of God's word. It is not for unknown reasons that Satan has been called a prowling lion in the Bible. Readers who doubt this can go back to the temptation of Jesus in the desert by Satan and see the skillful manipulation of the Biblical verses in the Psalms by Satan(**Psalm 91:11-12**), in a vain attempt to get Jesus to test His father by appealing to His power. Yes Satan knows the Scriptures well!

The World vs Israel, God and His Holy Ones
The Orthodox Jews will take arms and protect themselves successfully at first against the Arabs as did Israel in days past. The Antichrist will overthrow the first of the three horns prophesied by Daniel - the overseer in the Middle East and request help from the two overseers of Africa and Russia and the central republics, which they will decline, having been devastated in the last war against Israel. As Daniel sees in his vision, the Antichrist will then overthrow three regional overseers for insubordination, knowing his time to establish his kingdom is limited (exactly 3.5 years).

*"While I was thinking about the horns, there before me was another horn, a little one, which came up among them; and three of the first horns were uprooted before it. This horn had eyes like the eyes of a human being and a mouth that spoke boastfully" **Daniel 7:8** (NIV)*

Satan knows he must move quickly to destroy the rest of the Jews and preempt the Messiah from returning. Because the Messiah has indeed established conditions in **Matthew 23:29** for the Jews in order to return. If they don't want Him, He will not return. Its another thing if Satan has ensured that they are all destroyed before their eyes are opened to call on Him.

The Jews in Jerusalem are once again under existential threat, this time from the global soldiers from the New World Order assembled from different regions to enforce the peace. A war of take no prisoners is started against the remnant of the Orthodox Jews. Seeing the futility of defending, even to the last man against these global legions, it appears that the end of the road has finally arrived for the remnant of the Jews who have remained faithful to God. But the fate of the enemies of God has already been sealed.

The prophet Jeremiah gives us the fate of those who war against Israel, God and His hidden ones in line with Psalm 83 from Asaph:

*"At that time those slain by the LORD **will be everywhere**--from one end of the earth to the other. They will not be mourned or gathered up or buried, **but will be like dung lying on the ground." Jeremiah 25:33** (NIV)*

Finally, the Orthodox Jews will realize that with the whole world, a self-loathing progressive government and the remaining regional overseers against them, there is no escape even in Jerusalem. At this time, the verses regarding the Messiah Yehshua(Jesus) in the Torah will open to them and they will plead for help to God to send forth his Messiah to save them. Maybe they will even remember what Rabbi Yitzhak Kaduri told them not that long ago.

This final attempt at genocide in this corner of the world will be blacked out of the mainstream news media even as global soldiers sent by the overseers are fighting to finish off this threat to the Antichrist's full dominion on earth. With former enemies and soldiers from the ends of the earth arrayed against them, something that would have been impossible before the global unification following World War 3, the Savior will hear their cry and arrive to destroy the enemies arrayed against the Jews for their final destruction.

*"Now, brothers and sisters, about times and dates we do not need to write to you, for you know very well that the day of the Lord will come like a thief in the night. While people are saying, "Peace and safety," destruction will come on them suddenly, as labor pains on a pregnant woman, and they will not escape." **1 Thessalonians 5:1-2** (NIV)*

*"On that day his feet will stand on the Mount of Olives, east of Jerusalem, and the Mount of Olives will be split in two from east to west, forming a great valley, with half of the mountain moving north and half moving south." **Zechariah 14:4** (NIV)*

A great escape through the Lord's new valley as in times past

The Lord tells the Jewish and Christian believers in Jerusalem how they are to flee the global army through the mountain valley He creates all the way to Azel, just as the Israelites fled the Egyptians across the Red Sea through the Lord's valley in the midst of the sea and just as Lot fled the destruction of Sodom and Gommorah in ancient times through the angel's designated route to Zoar. As Zechariah tells us, the Lord will arrive with His Holy Ones and save His people in Israel, destroying the armies of the Beast's global overseers in Jerusalem.

"You will flee by my mountain valley, for it will extend to **Azel**. *You will flee as you fled from the earthquake in the days of Uzziah king of Judah.* **Then the Lord my God will come,** *and all the holy ones with him."* **Zechariah 14:5** *(NIV)*

The Israelis have officially named this Biblical valley Atzal or Nahal Atzal. The mouth of the valley lies at the base of the southernmost summit of the Mount of Olives or Mount of Corruption. Nahal Atzal is one of the tributaries of the Kidron Valley southeast of Jerusalem, between the Armon Hanatziv ridge and the neighborhood of Abu Tor, by the Peace Forest. (The Peace Forest itself stretches from Ancient Jerusalem to the Armon Hanatziv ridge). Nahal Atzal is currently only a riverbed, but that will change just before the Lord comes.

CHAPTER 13
Return of Messiah and the Saints

THE COMING OF MESSIAH had been expected from the time of Adam after the Fall. After His crucifixion and resurrection, the return of Jesus Christ to earth a second time to save the world has been expected and hoped for almost 2000 years by Christians.

"so Christ was sacrificed once to take away the sins of many; and he will appear a second time, not to bear sin, but to bring salvation to those who are waiting for him." **Hebrews 9:28** *(NIV)*

In 2030, we will mark the 2000th anniversary of His death and resurrection. By 2027, with the fulfillment of the singularity (AI) as predicted by Ray Kurzweil, the entire world will be under the control of Antichrist and individuals everywhere will be unable to resist his unlimited temporal power, on earth. Christ's Second Coming will be eagerly awaited by those believers who plan to ride out the tribulation in secret till He comes. Conservative believers will hide in the hills and woods and congregate to pray in secret away from the watchful eyes of drones and dust sized ubiquitous sixth generation communication networks.

However those who have accepted the kingdom of the Antichrist and his implants will suffer grievous harm in their bodies and these circuits are now shorted under the skin, causing them to itch and burn and turn into malignant sores. The fate of the wicked rulers on earth under the reign of Antichrist who think that peace and safety are theirs at least to do as they please will end just as quickly as just they settle down to a new Aquarian era of peace after beating down the Christians and attempting to wipe out Jews in a small corner of the world, out of sight. Indeed God herds the kings of the earth together and throws them into an everlasting prison. There are no exceptions made for any of the evil-doers, certainly not for any of the regional overseers or the Antichrist.

"In that day the Lord will punish the powers in the heavens above
  and the kings on the earth below.
  They will be herded together
  like prisoners bound in a dungeon;
  they will be shut up in prison
  and be punished after many days." *Isaiah 24:21-22* (NIV)

The sign by which each user in the kingdom is authenticated to buy, sell and live their lives is the sign by which he is punished just as Cain was punished in the beginning by God.

" The first angel went and poured out his bowl on the land, and ugly, festering sores broke out on the people who had the mark of the beast and worshiped its image." Revelation 16:2 (NIV)

When Jesus returns, the entire system of the Antichrist will collapse instantly. The hardened and massively intelligent quantum computer(QC) self destructs as the laws of physics themselves are changed by God, in a way that no bomb on earth could wipe out. With the breath of his lips, the Lord will slay the wicked(**Isaiah 11:4**). The wicked who accept the implant of the beast, oblivious till the end consuming fake news and living in a faked reality, will end up as ashes on the ground.

"At that time those slain by the LORD will be everywhere-- from one end of the earth to the other. They will not be mourned or gathered up or buried, but will be like dung lying on the ground." **Jeremiah 25:33** (NIV)

The prophet Jeremiah tells us that at this time the earth will be in complete darkness, just as in the beginning, when it was without form and void. For what light on the earth can exist without God who is the source of all light ? The darkness will be complete and all those who live on the earth, human and animal will be frightened in anticipation of the things to come. It will be like someone just switched off the light in the universe. This is just before Jesus soon arrives in glory, bringing His glorious light again to the world.

"I looked at the earth, and it was formless and empty; and at the heavens, and their light was gone." **Jeremiah 4:23** (NIV)

Gives a whole new meaning to that saying of our Lord, doesn't it ? (**John 8:12**). Those of us on earth will see what the Lord said in an entirely new light. It is literally true. Alleluia!

Jesus will arrive in His full glory and the whole world will get to see Him. When the Jews finally realize that the Messiah was the same one that was crucified, they will weep for Him whom they have pierced. They will then fathom the full depth of their ingratitude to God in times past with their whole being, just as the rest of us also will.

"And I will pour out on the house of David and the

*inhabitants of Jerusalem a spirit of grace and supplication. They will look on me, the one they have pierced, and they will mourn for him as one mourns for an only child, and grieve bitterly for him as one grieves for a firstborn son." **Zechariah 12:10** (NIV)*

*"Then will appear the sign of the Son of Man in heaven. And then all the peoples of the earth will mourn when they see the Son of Man coming on the clouds of heaven, with power and great glory. And he will send his angels with a loud trumpet call, and they will gather his elect from the four winds, from one end of the heavens to the other." **Matthew 24:30-31** (NIV)*

As the Bible states, most of the world will have absolutely no inkling of when Christ's return is imminent.

*"But about that day or hour no one knows, not even the angels in heaven, nor the Son, but only the Father." **Matthew 24:36** (NIV)*

You must remember that at this time there is also a worldwide news blackout by the mainstream media of the events going on in Jerusalem. Indeed the day of the Lord will come like a thief in the night for most of the world in their fake news reality.

"for you know very well that the day of the Lord will come like a thief in the night. While people are saying, "Peace and safety," destruction will come on them suddenly, as labor pains on a pregnant woman, and they will not escape." **2 Thessalonians 5:2-3** *(NIV)*

Most of the world continue eating, drinking, marrying and giving into marriage, throwing parties, going about their work oblivious of the real news around them, just as in the days of

Noah.

"It was the same in the days of Lot. People were eating and drinking, buying and selling, planting and building. But the day Lot left Sodom, fire and sulfur rained down from heaven and destroyed them all. It will be just like this on the day the Son of Man is revealed" **Luke 17:28-30** *(NIV)*

"As it was in the days of Noah, so it will be at the coming of the Son of Man." **Matthew 24:37** *(NIV)*

But *believing Christians* in the world at that time will know, both from counting down daily the limited time given to Antichrist and understanding that what they are shown on the news they are allowed to see is mostly faked, and will anticipate Christ's return. Christian survivors in Israel and especially in Jerusalem, the last desolate holdout against Antichrist, will especially know when His return is very close.

"But you, brothers and sisters, are not in darkness so that this day should surprise you like a thief. You are all children of the light and children of the day. We do not belong to the night or to the darkness." **1 Thessalonians 5:4-5** *(NIV)*

We will know. And the rest of the world too will then see the Lord coming in a cloud with great glory.

"People will faint from terror, apprehensive of what is coming on the world, for the heavenly bodies will be shaken. At that time they will see the Son of Man coming in a cloud with power and great glory. When these things begin to take place, stand up and lift up your heads, because your redemption is drawing near." **Luke 21:26-28** *(NIV)*

"Men of Galilee," they said, "why do you stand here looking into the sky? This same Jesus, who has been taken from you into heaven, will come back in the same way you have seen him go into heaven."" **Acts 1:11** *(NIV)*

Binding of Satan and a millennium of peace overseen by the Lord

Surviving Christians and the remnant of the Jews will rejoice to see the Lord. Christians will come out of their hiding places where they waited, away from the forced cybernetic implants of the Antichrist and see his destruction at the hands of the Lord.

"And he seized the dragon, that ancient serpent, who is the devil and Satan, and bound him for a thousand years, and threw him into the pit, and shut it and sealed it over him, so that he might not deceive the nations any longer, until the thousand years were ended. After that he must be released for a little while.

Then I saw thrones, and seated on them were those to whom the authority to judge was committed. Also I saw the souls of those who had been beheaded for the testimony of Jesus and for the word of God, and those who had not worshiped the beast or its image and had not received its mark on their foreheads or their hands. They came to life and reigned with Christ for a thousand years. The rest of the dead did not come to life until the thousand years were ended. This is the first resurrection." **Revelation 20:2-5** *(NIV)*

Let us then remain faithful to Christ till the end so that we may lift up our heads before Him when our Redemption appears, just as John also tells us.

"And now, dear children, continue in him, so that when he

*appears we may be confident and unashamed before him at his coming." **1 John 2:28** (NIV)*

Maranatha, Even so, Come Lord Jesus!

CHAPTER 14
A New Millennium

WITH THE REMOVAL of the last of the evildoers and the final destruction of the abhorrent corporatocratic and so-called *humanistic* world system, the world will be peaceful for the next 1000 years after the return of Christ. The Lord's temple restored and resplendent will beckon all good people of the earth to learn the law and the word of the Lord. There will be no more wars or training for wars. Altruism will return to mens' hearts. They will again look out for each other in a spirit of compassion and truth. Humor aside - lies, deception and fake news will no longer be found anywhere, at least for a thousand glorious years.

> *"In the last days*
> *the mountain of the Lord's temple will be established*
> *as the highest of the mountains;*
> *it will be exalted above the hills,*
> *and all nations will stream to it.*
> *Many peoples will come and say,*
> *"Come, let us go up to the mountain of the Lord,*
> *to the temple of the God of Jacob.*
> *He will teach us his ways,*
> *so that we may walk in his paths."*
> *The law will go out from Zion,*
> *the word of the Lord from Jerusalem.*
> *He will judge between the nations*

and will settle disputes for many peoples.
They will beat their swords into plowshares
and their spears into pruning hooks.
Nation will not take up sword against nation,
nor will they train for war anymore." **Isaiah 2:2-4**
(NIV)

We who have not received the beast's implants inside our foreheads or our hands, who have been faithful to Jesus, once promised mansions by Him will also get our own spanking new thrones! We will live and reign with Him for a thousand years. Death will no longer sting nor win over our glorious bodies given to us by the Lord.

"And I saw thrones, and they sat upon them, and judgment was given unto them: and I saw the souls of them that were beheaded for the witness of Jesus, and for the word of God, and which had not worshipped the beast, neither his image, neither had received his mark upon their foreheads, or in their hands; and they lived and reigned with Christ a thousand years." **Revelation 20:4** *(NIV)*

The changes that will come upon the world with the return of Jesus Christ that have been alluded to at other places in the Bible will not be revisited here. Suffice it to say, Time is a scroll and changes will bring the earth once again to the time in the garden of Eden when creation was ordered, not disordered as it is today. But that is the subject of another book. Our God is an awesome God!

"Remember the former things, those of long ago;
I am God, and there is no other;
I am God, and there is none like me.

I make known the end from the beginning,
  from ancient times, what is still to come.
I say, 'My purpose will stand,
  and I will do all that I please.'" **Isaiah 46:9-10** *(NIV)*

BONUS CHAPTER: The Beast and the Seven Kings

In May 1966, at the height of the Cold War, a weary old man shuffled up in front of Congress and offered his testimony before the U.S. Senate Internal Security Subcommittee, where he stripped to the waist to show 18 scars from torture wounds covering his body. This man's name was Rev. Richard Wurmbrand and he was the Romanian founder of the "Voice of the Martyrs" ministry, a voice for nameless persecuted Christians around the world. In September 1966, he was warned that Romania's Communist regime planned to assassinate him, but he would not be silenced. He had been in prison for a total of 13 years under the Communist regime and he had the scars to prove it. He told the Committee:

"When I was out from prison in 1956, I was licensed to preach – of course, nobody can preach in our country accept he has a license from the Government – and in the beginning I got a license, but which was withdrawn from me after the first week of preaching. This was because I was preaching that communism will change, that communism will fall." And the communists were telling him "Never will it fall." The communists reproached him for speaking in a sermon that "Christians must practice patience, patience, and again patience. The Americans will come and we must be patient until they come."

He tells us something interesting about Jesus's Ministry that he did not understand until he had his own ministry to his fellow countrymen.

"I did not understand in earlier times why Jesus, when He wishes to have the last supper said: "Go in town and you will see a man with a pitcher and go after him and where he enters prepare the supper."

"Why does he not give an address, a number, and a street?

Now we know it when we make secret prayer meetings. We never give the address. We don't know if that man is not the informer of the secret police. We tell to the man to wait in a public garden or somewhere, and when one with a flower here, or with a necktie passes, go after him."

Like the apostle Paul before him, he describes his physical condition in dealing with the godless people of his time "I have much more broken bones than anybody, so either I broke my bones or somebody else broke them."

As the world's most prominent atheist Richard Dawkins argues in his book "The God Delusion", why there is almost "certainly" no God and Christians are only weak minds with "god" delusions, so said the "astute" and "virtuous" (*their own words*) atheist Communists before him. Yet the Soviet Union is no more and Christianity is still flourishing despite being the most persecuted religion worldwide. And Tertullian explains this phenomenon well, writing in 197 AD "*The blood of martyrs is the seed of the church*". To Dawkins and others, we are still fools for Christ but as the apostle Paul stated(**1 Corinthians 4:10**), we're proud to carry that label!

The Seven Kings of Revelation

For a long enough time, Christian scholars have debated the seven heads of the Beast or seven kings of Revelation 17(these are not the ten horns of the Beast that are also ten kings with the little horn that we explained in a previous chapter). We know there is literally no creature with seven heads so in this case we can take this beast as a symbol. A symbol does not have to refer to one and only one thing. Here Scripture itself tells us that the heads refer both to seven mountains and seven kings, meaning the symbol has multiple fulfillments.

For example, we have the fulfillment twice in history of a powerful godless empire aka the Beast burning the whore or prostitute Jerusalem. The uneasy alliance between the Roman empire and Jerusalem that trampled underfoot the Jewish and Christian people of God broke down in A.D. 66-70, when Rome and its allied forces conquered Israel and then destroyed, sacked, and burned Jerusalem, just as Jesus prophesied (*Luke 21:5–24*). At the time of Antichrist, this occurs again this time with ten horns in league with the Beast.

The difficulty has been in placing the seven kings among seven successive Roman emperors in what was expected to be a reference to the Roman empire at the time. However it is likely the Apostle John is also not really talking about the very *first* seven emperors as is evident with his writing of the martyrdom of Antipas at the time of Domitian*(Revelation 2:13)*. And that mention of Antipas by John places the book of Revelation squarely in the period from 81-96 AD when Domitian reigned as emperor.

The fact that Christians and Jews were believers in One God prevented Christians and Jews from participating in anything involving other gods. Christians did not offer sacrifices or offer worship to the gods and this made the Romans more hostile. While the previous two Roman emperors were not deified until after they were dead, that changed with the coming of the emperor Caligula. From Caligula onwards those living in the Roman territories were required to offer incense to the living Roman emperor, and in the minds of the people, the emperor, when viewed as a god, was the embodiment of the empire, so Christians were seen as disloyal to Rome and their "god".

We must note that during the reigns of Augustus and Tiberius, Jews and Christians were not persecuted by the Romans. Judaea was a client state under the Romans ruled by Herod and the Jewish temple was free to conduct its activities without interference from Rome. The client state was only required to pay taxes to Rome and pledge allegiance to the Roman emperor.

However from the time of Caligula(37-41 AD), persecutions began in earnest against the followers of the living God. It is said that Caligula was so wicked that he commanded himself to be worshipped as God, and temples to be built in his name. He sat in these temples among the gods, requiring that his image be set up in all temples and he threatened to do so also in the Temple at Jerusalem, which caused a great disturbance among the Jews, but this threatened abomination was not carried out.

Now counting from this first Roman emperor to declare himself a "living god" in direct opposition to the living God of Abraham, Issac and Jacob, the infamous Domitian is the sixth, if you discount the stunningly brief reigns of Galba, Otho and Vitellius, all of who came to power in a period of months. Galba, Otho and Vitellius were all military leaders involved in campaigns mostly in Europe(Spain and Portugal, far away from Palestine) and were also all deposed in the same year (69 AD).

In 69 AD, Vespasian who had been sent by Nero along with his son Titus to quell the rebellion in Jerusalem(66-70AD) became Roman emperor as he successfully waited for Galba, Otho and Vitellius to dispatch each other in Europe, finishing with the last, Vitellius himself. John could have blinked and not seen these three as they were all gone almost as soon as they came to power. It is likely that at Rome's time of widespread anarchy(68-69AD) after Nero's suicide in 68AD, John sees only General Vespasian who is conducting the campaign against Jerusalem with his son Titus and later becomes emperor. So here is a likely list of the 7 kings that John is referring to:

(1) Caligula (37-41 AD, first emperor to declare himself a living god and begin persecution of Jews and Christians)

(2) Claudius (41-54 AD)

(3) Nero (54-68AD)

(4) Vespasian (69-79AD, 69 AD being "Year of the 4 emperors" - Galba, Otho, Vitellius and Vespasian, the first three

who do not appear to be alluded to by John)

(5) Titus (79-81AD)

(6) Domitian (81-96AD)

(7) Nerva (September 96-January 98AD) - the "good" emperor

So the five fake living "gods" that have "fallen" against the God of heaven at the time of John's writing, in their direct war against the living God become Caligula, Claudius, Nero, Vespasian and Titus. At the time of the apostle John's writing, Domitian is the sixth *who is,* and then comes one of a very short reign, Nerva who is considered one of the "good" Roman emperors in that he did not severely persecute Christians.

Just as the prophet Daniel stops at Antiochus Epiphanes and continues again from Gog, the apostle John does not take up from after Nerva but comes again to the Beast who is of a later time and age. Then the Apostle offers no more Roman emperors in the list who persecute Christians - there are many, just like there are many after Antiochus Epiphanes against the Jews seen by the prophet Daniel.

Instead John talks of a Beast who is like the seven mentioned Roman emperors, and is from the same self-proclaimed "god" stock as they are. If you look closely, the apostle is referring to parallels in not only his age but also in the modern age just before Christ returns. Hence the multiply fulfilled symbolism of the seven heads or kings. There is another empire clearly such as this, only more recent.

The last godless global Empire

A godless persecuting empire of a recent age that fits perfectly into the apostle John's vision much like the Roman empire is the ex-Soviet Union. Just like the Roman empire before it, the stability of the Soviet state accept no religious rival for the allegiance of its subjects. The state was the highest good in a union of state and state allowed religion that placed its own leader as worthy of reverence in every home or allowed no religion at all.

At its worst, it is estimated that of 50,000 churches of Russian Orthodox faith there were less than 500 remaining at the time of Stalin who ordered priests and seminarians shot on the spot or exiled to gulags to serve hard labor. Stalin who actually started in a Russian orthodox seminary embraced Marxism, later became a bank robber and started his purge of the Church in earnest at the side of Lenin who found him a most willing accomplice in his attempt to stamp God out of the public square.

Again in the Soviet Union, there is a perfect match with John's vision in the number of godless Bolshevik "emperors" - who are exactly seven in number including Konstantin Chernenko widely considered in communist circles as the "last Bolshevik", while Mikhail Gorbachev, the eighth is widely derided in the same circles as the destroyer of the Soviet Union.

If you look carefully, you will find amazing parallels in militant atheism in the West today and that practiced in the Soviet Union in the last century. The ideology of Marxism-Leninism upheld this doctrine advocating the abolition of religion and the propagation of atheism. Government officials worked tirelessly to sanitize the public sphere of any trace of religion.

The way militant atheism worked in practice was very methodical. In 1918, the Union of Soviet Socialist Republics, under Lenin, implemented a policy of separation of Church and State, which meant that all Church property (including monasteries, charitable and social works and even liturgical items) was nationalized without compensation.

Orthodox priests, monks and nuns were taken away to the Gulag and often times executed. Pastors, priests and seminarians were dispatched whether by firing squad, being sent to "corrective labor" camps, or to psychiatric hospitals for "treatment," most never to be seen again.

Several thousand churches of all Christian denominations were either closed, liquidated or forcibly converted into "Museums of Atheism." In addition, religious schools were closed and the teaching of religion to minors was outlawed. The total number of Christian victims killed under the Soviet regime has been estimated to range between 14-22 million.

Militant atheism became central to the ideology of the Communist Party of the Soviet Union and a high priority policy of all Soviet leaders. Convinced atheists were considered to be more politically astute and *virtuous* individuals. The state established atheism as the only scientific truth. Soviet authorities forbade the criticism of atheism and the state's anti-religious policies.

In practice the state also sought to control religious bodies and to interfere with them, with the ultimate goal of making them disappear, similar to what is done in China even today. To this effect, the state sought to control the activities of different religious communities, not just Christian. Muslims were also singled out.

Do you see parallels in the West even in the United States here, in the not so recent past ? Many religious were also subjected to psychological punishment or torture and mind control experimentation in order to force them to give up their religious convictions. The practice was aptly called "Punitive psychiatry".

During the first five years of Soviet power, the Bolsheviks executed Russian Orthodox bishops and over 1,200 Russian Orthodox priests. Many others were imprisoned or exiled. Patriarch Tikhon of Moscow excommunicated the Soviet leadership on January 19, 1918 for conducting this campaign. In retaliation the regime arrested and killed dozens of bishops, thousands of the lower clergy and monastics, and multitudes of laity.

The old Marxist assumption that religion would disappear

on its own with changing material conditions was challenged as religion persisted. The Soviet leadership still debated how best to combat religion. The positions ranged from the belief that religion would die on its own naturally with increasing education, to that which demanded that religion be attacked ruthlessly till it was destroyed.

Let us take a look at the leaders of the Soviet Union for all of the years it existed from the October Revolution in 1917 -1991. You will find stunning parallels between this empire and the Roman empire in the first century AD of the time the apostle was speaking. They are as follows:

(1) Vladimir Lenin (1922-24)

The first leader of the Soviet Union after the October revolution was Vladimir Lenin. Lenin called the struggle to disseminate atheism 'the cause of our state'.

(2) Joseph Stalin (1924-1953)

Josef Stalin stated flatly in the 1930s that, "God must be out of Russia in five years." But by loosening up on religious freedom during World War 2, Stalin also served his objective of favorably impressing the Allies. He was aware that a good part of the anti-Soviet sentiment in the West, especially in the United States, was because of the persecution of the church. On June 23, 1941, Roosevelt had actually compared the lack of religious freedom in Nazi Germany to that of Soviet Russia, equating the two.

In order to demonstrate that state-imposed atheism was a thing of the past, Soviet representatives were sent to the Allied powers to provide assurances about the Communist change of direction. Foreign religious leaders were invited to visit Moscow, and Stalin himself told the English ambassador that, in his own way, he believed in God. Well Stalin wasn't exactly lying, because he started as a seminarian!

In America few Christians believed in Stalin's "conversion," considering it a political move. True to form after winning the war against Nazi Germany, Stalin went into full religious repression mode, having tens of millions of his fellow citizens tortured or killed for professing their faith.

(3) Georgy Malenkov (1953-1955)

Personal connections with Vladimir Lenin sped his rise in the Soviet leadership. By 1925, he was entrusted with overseeing the party's records. This brought him into contact with Stalin, then the de-facto leader of the Soviet Union. As a result of this association, Malenkov became heavily involved in Stalin's infamous purges. As Premier, Malenkov remained the nation's foremost policymaker until being removed from power in 1955 by Nikita Khrushchev, the Party's First Secretary.

(4) Nikita Khruschev (1955-1964)

But in 1959 Nikita Khrushchev initiated his own campaign against the Russian Orthodox Church and forced the closure of about 12,000 churches. By 1985 fewer than 7,000 churches remained active. Members of the church hierarchy were jailed or forced out, their places taken by docile clergy, many of whom had ties with the KGB! Under Khruschev, the Pentecostals were singled out as a group to be banned completely from the Soviet Union along with Jehovah's witnesses. That was in no less part to their perceived religious zeal in which they were gaining converts from among the communists.

(5) Leonid Brezhnev (1964-1982)

After the harsh treatment under Khrushchev believers may have derived some hope from the period of drift in Soviet religious policy that followed his fall in October 1964. The number of anti-religious press articles began to decrease and their tone became less offensive. In practical terms this change was reflected in the release of nearly 200 Baptist prisoners and, in some cases, the removal of their state sentences.

The Soviet communist propogandist rued the fact that the Russian Orthodox Church, allegedly the preserve of the ignorant "babushka"(old women), was proving increasingly attractive to young intellectuals who had become disillusioned with the official communist ideology. Yes, the communists still believed that nihilism(the belief that life is meaningless) was very attractive to the human being! From such young people began the Christian Seminar, and many other study groups, which sought to explore the meaning of Christ in the modern world.

(6) Yuri Andropov(1982-1984)

It was under his chairmanship of the KGB that even more assaults upon religious dissent was launched and the number of special psychiatric prison hospitals rose from three to **thirty**. However Andropov being more aware of the pressing social and economic problems facing Soviet society, did not directly attack Christian believers as Stalin had done. For him was the old way of "punitive psychiatry" with more appropriate "hospital" care.

(7) Konstantin Chernenko, **the last Bolshevik** (1984-1985)

Even as late as 1984, Soviet premier Konstantin Chernenko vowed to "protect the ideological purity of young people against the pernicious taint of religion." As attendance at Soviet churches began increasing, Chernenko asked the politburo to agree to his measures to restrict church attendance. Chernenko died a *little more than a year* of gaining ascendancy to the Soviet politburo.

This extremely short "reign" of the seventh godless "emperor" just before the end of the Soviet Union again appears to be a modern double fulfillment of **Revelation 17:10,** this time in the greatest godless empire of the 20th century, that is symbolized by the Beast of Revelation.

"They are also seven kings. Five have fallen, one is, the other has not yet come; **but when he does come, he must remain for only a little while." Revelation 17:10** (NIV)

In all respects, Chernenko was the last Bolshevik, the last of the seven kings of a revived Roman empire of the modern age, the godless Soviet empire. With the end of the last Bolshevik after a very short "reign", came forth the mild mannered socialist Mikhail Gorbachev bringing the gifts of perestroika(reforms with end of central planning), glasnost(open government and open information) and the inevitable end of the Soviet Union. Religious minded successive politicians in Russia with some more help from the United States and the West as well as the uprisings in the satellite states of the Iron curtain dissolved and ended the Soviet Union with its socialist republics and its many East European satellite vassals.

Yet just as in Nero's Roman Empire, Christianity in the Soviet Union neither disappeared, nor was it much weakened, by decades of persecution, as Tertullian too had observed in the Roman empire of the 2nd century AD. The character, loyal community, and sincere belief of Russian Christians enabled them to maintain their faith and even to gain additional followers despite all the efforts of the Soviet government to eliminate them.

Would Gorbachev have eventually become the Beast of Revelation as the eighth "emperor", given the opportunity and if Communism had covered the entire earth ? It is difficult to say. Certainly Moscow too can claim to be built on seven hills just like Rome but this is considered an exaggeration today considering its geography. However the extent to which this city spread godlessness throughout the world in such a short time can scarcely be exaggerated. Its repercussions are felt even today in the United States, once the last remaining stand against Communism, along with the United Kingdom.

Following the history of God's patient treatment of Israel, it could be that God decided to give humanity one more chance before the Beast makes his appearance. Additionally the rest of the events we discussed in earlier chapters politically, socially, demographically and technologically had not yet lined up for global dominance of any one kingdom. Mankind should consider this as a reprieve from the heavens. Yet it appears instead that Mankind has employed this brief reprieve to even more firmly embrace the godless and immoral ways of Noah's generation before the Flood.

Consider this last empire that once covered 60% of the earth's countries as a warning from God Himself of the things to come again 40 years later. The next time the Beast came in a newer version of the revived Roman empire, his kingdom would be 100% global as laid out in the previous chapters.

The Eighth king, the Beast who is of the seven

As you have seen in previous chapters, The Beast who is to come in the next decade has characteristics of all the first seven godless Roman emperors of the 1st century as well as the seven godless Soviet leaders who oversaw the ruthless Communist empire of the 20th century, before its fall. Neither communist China, Cuba or Venezuela or any others have had this global impact. The second beast seeing the futility of all out violence against humanity will now take the characteristics of a lamb while espousing this same godless religion. The apostle John describes him as talking like a lamb while having the characteristics of a dragon. He comes in cunning and stealth, winning over the people with charm and sweet talk but starts to unveil his agenda only once he is enthroned.

"Then I saw a second beast, coming out of the earth. It had two horns like a lamb, **but** *it spoke like a dragon. "*
Revelation 13:11 *(NIV)*

The closest parallel to such a leader is the "lamb-like" progressive humanist of today. Yet behind the scenes, this two-horned lamb acts like a dragon. It is from this ideology that the Second Beast will emerge, mocking God and winning over people to his kingdom. The Roman emperors as well as the Soviet emperors failed to win people over by force and the Beast understands this well today, because the Beast is in league with a force that is older than man. He is animated by the prince of deceivers, Satan himself.

The Beast, Rome and Jerusalem

The beast will be the leader of the ten overseers of the regions discussed in the previous chapters. And the global headquarters of the humanist anti-God Beast is still Rome, even if you follow past history and the fact that it is a 100% global version of the godless revived Roman empire complete with the original city of the seven hills as its headquarters. Mystery Babylon as proven in a previous chapter is still Jerusalem.

The anti-God Beast and the new ultra-progressive government in Jerusalem however work together for "peace" in the Middle East as we previously discussed, after World War 3 ends. The final trap of the Antichrist for the physical remnant of the Jews is in place after progressive humanist governments everywhere else stifle true Christian faith and favor only heretics that support their policies, just as in the past.

And you will be able to identify the Antichrist in advance as an internationally popular smooth talking anti-God progressive humanist who takes the first mark of the Beast to himself, the same implant that was so clearly identified in previous chapters.

While the following is personal speculation, you may identify him as a politician who has had prior experience with mind altering drugs so that a more powerful brain implant that operates in a similar manner may be something that he will not fear of employing even in himself and to his ends, in order to build his new kingdom of willing acolytes.

Return to the beginning after Creation

The godless religion of Man described in these chapters is not
new. It began just after the creation of the First Man with a lie. We
are told that this lie was first offered by Satan to Eve and through
Eve, to her husband Adam.

*"You will not certainly die," the serpent said to the woman.
"For God knows that when you eat from it your eyes will be
opened, and you will be like God, knowing good and evil."*
Genesis 3:4-5 *(NIV)*

So in Genesis we have the first promise of humanism or self
received "enlightenment" with mortal Man as his own supreme
God. Mankind was promised that they would become as gods by
their own efforts, without having God Himself in them, something
that Jesus has freely offered us through the Ages.

Today, in the age of science and technology, Satan's original
lie has been repackaged. The ideas are dressed up in new terms
such as spiritual evolution through Gnostic knowledge and self-
experimentation and physical evolution through globally
connected artificial intelligence to begin a *New Age of
enlightenment.* Yet it is still the same age old lie Satan told Eve
and Adam.

A connection again between events on Christmas 1990 and a year later, Christmas 1991

Just as the events on the day after Christmas 2003 and a year
later, the day after Christmas 2004 discussed earlier in this book,
a believer who looks closely at two seemingly unconnected earth-
shaking events, one on Christmas 1990 and the other occurring on
the day after Christmas 1991 may see only a coincidence in the
dates.

The day after Christmas 1991, a tumultuous political event took place in the history of mankind - the formal dissolution of the Soviet Union. A year earlier on Christmas 1990, at CERN(The European Organization for Nuclear Research), the world-wide web(WWW) was quietly birthed with the first successful communication on the web. This demonstration was followed by several more years of technological progress that would soon forever change the world of human communication right down to the present day, and eventually in the next decade connect humanity together to the final Beast of Revelation. Of course, the scientists at CERN know nothing about the Beast - that was not their initial goal. Coincidence ? Or just another example of God trying to warn Man of what is to come ? From what you've read so far, what do you think ?

References

Flavius Josephus, The Wars of the Jews, William Whiston, A.M., Ed.

Ancient Christian Commentary on Scripture, Isaiah 40-66 (IVP press 2007; Mark W. Elliott, Ph.d., Cambridge)

The Prophecy of Daniel: A Commentary, Edward J. Young, 1977

The Return of the Lord, John F. Walvoord, 1983

Foes from the Northern Frontier Dr. Edwin Yamauchi, 2003

The Book of Ezekiel, Daniel I. Block, 1998

Club of Rome, "Limits to Growth" 1972, First through Fifth printings, a report for the Club of Rome's project on the Predicament of Mankind

Club of Rome, "Regionalized and Adaptive Model of the Global World System", September 1973, a report for the Club of Rome's project on the Predicament of Mankind

Testimony of Rev. Richard Wurmbrand, Friday, May 6, 1966, Hearing before the subcommittee to investigate the administration of the Internal Security Act and other internal security laws of the committee on the judiciary, United States Senate, Eighty-ninth Congress (Second session)

Glossary

Aisha - last and youngest wife of the Prophet Mohammad

AI - Artificial Intelligence

IA - Intelligence amplification, also referred to as cognitive augmentation or machine augmented intelligence

antichrist - One of many deceivers out to deceive the followers of God into apostasy preceding the final Antichrist.

Antichrist - (Capitalized in the book), the last demonic deceiver to come in as mentioned in the Book of Revelation at the end of times

Byzantine - Orthodox Christian empire in Asia Minor, superseded by Islamic Turkey

Caliph - leader of the Muslims

CPC - Communist Party of China, founding and sole governing party of the People's Republic of China

CoR - Club of Rome, international think-tank that deals with global challenges facing humanity started in Rome and now based in Winterthur, Switzerland. In the 1970s, it created a global computer model with help from an international team of researchers at the Massachusetts Institute of Technology(MIT) to determine alternative patterns for mankind's future.

Club of Madrid - a child organization of the Club of Rome along with the Club of Budapest. Composed of 95 regular members, 64 of whom are former presidents and 39 of whom are former prime ministers from 65 countries. The Club of Madrid is the world's largest forum of former heads of state and government.

Corporatocracy - a society or system that is governed or controlled by corporations.

Cybernetics - Electronic and / or mechanical based Control

DARPA - US Advanced Research Projects Agency

EU - European Union

Fatima - daughter of the Prophet Mohammad. In all three sons and four daughters were born to Mohammad. All Mohammad's children, except Fatima, died before him. So it is through Fatimah that Muhammad's lineage continued.

Gaia - the personification of the Earth and one of the Greek primordial deities. Gaia is the ancestral mother of all life: the primal Mother Earth goddess, hence also used as a modern reference to "Mother Earth"

Gnosticism - a prominent heretical movement of the 2nd-century Christian Church, partly of pre-Christian origin. Gnostic doctrine taught that the world was created and ruled by a lesser divinity, the demiurge, and that Christ was only one of many emissaries of the remote supreme divine being, esoteric or "hidden" knowledge of whom enabled the redemption of the human spirit

Gnostic Gospels - gospels that claim to reveal hidden messages of Jesus Christ. Not part of the four canonical gospels of Mathew, Mark, Luke and John, also penned in later centuries by unknown sources.

Gog and Magog - interchangeably used in the Bible to denote a leader that begins a world war either against the Jews before the Second Coming of Christ or believers of God on earth after the 1000 years of peace following the Second Coming

Hadith - sayings of the prophet Mohammad. There are several hadiths based on the source, like Sahih Bukhari, Sahih Muslim, etc

Hellenistic - relating to Greek history, language and culture

Khadija - first wife of the prophet Mohammad.

Mahdi - The Islamic rightly guided caliph who unites all Muslims

Messiah - promised deliverer of the Jewish nation. Christians and Muslims consider Jesus to be the Jewish Messiah.

NATO - North Atlantic Treaty Organization

Neurocybernetics - Brain control usually employing electronic implants in the brain

Nietzsche - Noted German philosopher and cultural critic, known for his tirades against religion and Christian morality, declared the "death of God". Modern nihilism is typically associated with him

Nihilism - the rejection of all religious and moral principles, in the belief that life is meaningless.

Occult - knowledge of the esoteric or the hidden, originating from ancient times, now clubbed under the umbrella of the "New Age"

Occulted - hidden (when used in reference to the Shiite Mahdi)

Paranoia - Having delusions of imminent harm, (adj) paranoid

Psychoactive - Substances that are prescribed for mental conditions such as depression or paranoia.

Rapture - A time when believers are caught up in the air to meet the Lord. Generally deemed to be before the Second Coming of Jesus Christ. Today pre-tribulation, mid-tribulation, post tribulation and prewrath rapture are also discussed based on when the time of the Rapture fits into the time line of the end of the age and the Second Coming.

Singularity - A point where the current laws of physics cease to operate as normal or exist, example a black hole or (in this book) with reference to humanity - the invention of super-intelligence causing unfathomable changes in human history

Shia - Muslims who believe the rightful successor of

Mohammad is his son-in-law Ali and disregard the three caliphs or companions of the Prophet.

Shiite - of the Shia

Sunnah or Sunnan - is the verbally transmitted record of the teachings, deeds and sayings of the Prophet Mohammad. Form an integral part of Muslim beliefs along with the Quran.

Sunni - Muslims who believe the successors of the Prophet are the first Islamic caliphs after Mohammad

Swedenborgian - of the church of the mystic Emanuel Swedenborg. Swedenborg was considered a heretic as he denied the holy trinity and the doctrine of blood atonement.

Teutonic - of the Teutons, a class of German Catholic knights founded in Acre, kingdom of Jerusalem in 1190 AD

Theosophy - movement founded in 1875 by Helena Blavatsky maintaining that a knowledge of God may be achieved through spiritual ecstasy, direct intuition, or special individual relations

Transhumanism - Modification by which humans can surpass their biological limitations usually with electronic or cybernetic implants

Tribulation - A time of trouble for believers before the second Coming of Christ.

Quran - Holy Book of the Muslims

Waraqah bin Nawfal - Nestorian Christian cousin (twice removed) of Mohammad and the first to believe in his prophethood.

WWW - The world wide web, started in the early 1990s as a set of interconnected computers at DARPA and today encompasses all sizes and shapes of interconnected devices that every other devices can communicate, download from or upload information to.

Notes

1

From the Dictionary of Dieties and Demons in the Bible
By Karen van der Toom, Bob Becking, Pieter Willem van
der Horst

2

It is vastly estimated that after WWII, the sex ratio in
Russia had dropped to 0.7 in favor of females! (Russia lost
20 million citizens in WWII). In the United States, the ratio
was not as skewed but still flipped at 0.85. Women's
suffrage denied to them till the 1920s was realized fully only
much later by re-enfranchizing poorer sections of society, a
disproportionate number of whom were poor women, by the
abolition of the poll tax in the 1960s. By the time of the new
liberals, the baby boomers had more or less restored the
gender ratio to parity

About the Author

Peter Jensen is a devoted follower of the Lord Jesus Christ. He likes traveling and experiencing new cultures, having lived in more than 15 countries in his lifetime. He has had a long career in technology, yet never losing his burning zeal for the Lord. He continues to cherish his many friendships with his fellow Christian apologetics. He and his wife live in Dallas, Texas.

Made in the USA
Lexington, KY
25 June 2019